S0-BIK-170

The Master Musicians

New Series Edited by Eric Blom

FAURÉ

UNIFORM WITH THIS VOLUME

BACH	Eva Mary and Sydney Grew
BARTÓK	Colin Mason
BEETHOVEN	Marion M. Scott
BERLIOZ	J. H. Elliot
BIZET	Winton Dean
BRAHMS	Peter Latham
CHOPIN	Arthur Hedley
DEBUSSY	Edward Lockspeiser
DVOŘÁK	Alec Robertson
ELGAR	Diana McVeagh
GLUCK	Alfred Einstein
HANDEL	Percy M. Young
HAYDN	Rosemary Hughes
MENDELSSOHN	Philip Radcliffe
MOZART	Eric Blom
MUSSORGSKY	M. D. Calvocoressi
PALESTRINA	Henry Coates
PURCELL	J. A. Westrup
RAVEL	Norman Demuth
SCHUBERT	Arthur Hutchings
SCHUMANN	Joan Chissell
STRAUSS	William Mann
TCHAIKOVSKY	Martin Cooper
VERDI	Dyneley Hussey
WAGNER	Robert L. Jacobs
WEBER	William Saunders

Gabriel Fauré

The Master Musicians

FAURÉ

by

NORMAN SUCKLING

Illustrated

Pellegrini & Cudahy, New York

1951

FIRST PUBLISHED IN THE U.S.A.
BY PELLEGRINI & CUDAHY 1951

PRINTED IN GREAT BRITAIN

CONTENTS

ILLUSTRATIONS

These illustrations are reproduced from *Gabriel Fauré*, by Ph. Fauré-Fremiet (Presses Universitaires de France).

CHAPTER I

INTRODUCTORY

To the best of my knowledge this is the first full-length study of Gabriel Fauré to be written in English. Admittedly he was a composer whose work had in the first place a more immediate appeal to his own countrymen than elsewhere; in this he resembles Elgar, as also in the fact that there is no real reason why the appreciation of him should never spread beyond his native land. Even in France, however, the literature concerning him is not extensive; it consists mainly of single chapters in works of more general reference, or articles in periodicals. The most important book relating purely to Fauré which has yet appeared is that by his devoted pupil, Charles Koechlin, in the *Maîtres de la Musique* series which also includes Pirro's *Bach* and Vincent d'Indy's *César Franck.* Two years after its publication there came another book by the composer's son, Philippe Fauré-Fremiet, containing less critical writing on the works but a much fuller biography—the author having been able to draw on a great many of Fauré's own letters—and copiously illustrated from a variety of sources. Other writing on him is chiefly of a kind to be consulted with regard to one or another particular department of his work: *e.g.* Vladimir Jankélévitch's book on the songs, consistently though this author relates his special study with the rest of Fauré's compositions.

In England, and elsewhere outside France, it is still possible to confuse him with his contemporary Jean-Baptiste Faure (written without the accent), a baritone singer and the composer of several songs which have attained a celebrity somewhat beyond their merits. The best-known of these, *Les Rameaux*, was attributed to Gabriel Fauré in a gramophone catalogue as late as 1941; and in his younger days the same confusion was liable to occur in France itself. To be sure, the two names are in essence the same; they derive ultimately from the Latin

*

word *faber* which appears elsewhere in French nomenclature as Fabre or Favre and farther north as Lefèvre—thus corresponding to our Smith or Wright; and the acute accent simply indicates the southern habit of vocalizing an atonic E. In its unaccented form the name has been that of numerous persons of varying renown in French history, including a President of the Republic; and as the form used by the composer's family is by far the less frequent, there is perhaps some excuse for the confusion.

Nevertheless Fauré's name, and his music, ought to be better known among us. It is not a creditable reflexion that even two major wars with Germany as our main enemy have still not cured us of the always harmful practice of drawing our musical principles from German sources; especially when one considers that the German primacy in music was manifested first in an artistically cosmopolitan age when German art was still permeated by Mediterranean influences, and that as soon as this primacy began to assume a properly national form it was productive of nothing but ill. In October 1922 the Paris *Revue musicale* issued a special Fauré number, which arrived in England at a time when French music could almost hope for a fair hearing; yet even then, in reviewing it for the *Musical Times*, M. D. Calvocoressi had to treat Fauré's reputation as still to be won in this country, a reservation which he would certainly not have had to make in the case of Richard Strauss or even Reger. Calvocoressi's discerning advocacy did not carry the weight it deserved; so that to this day our musical background is the poorer for not having incorporated, as one of its permanent features, the composer of a body of pianoforte music challenging Chopin's; a hundred songs, the best of which stand at least on a level with the highest achievements of the *Lieder*-writers; a handful of chamber works as good as any of Brahms; and the finest Requiem Mass since Mozart.

Fauré has an equal right with Debussy, though on somewhat different grounds, to be considered the greatest representative in music of what we may conveniently label in French history as the Third-Republic culture. This phase of French civilization was, as regards music, almost as much a rebirth as the early twentieth century was for England; not quite as much, since the barren period did not extend so far back, and its sterility, being traceable to rather different causes, was not so complete. During the sixty or more years subsequent to the Franco-Prussian war, Paris was more indubitably the centre of European culture than at any other time since the eighteenth century; a fact to which proper importance was never attached in music as it was in the other arts, with the result that Fauré's music was not only denied to be worthy of the same influence outside France as the painting of Cézanne or the poetry of Mallarmé, but in fact never exerted it. Yet his real value is commensurate with that of the other artists I have named; chiefly because he was a civilized composer with an adult outlook in an age liable to be attacked at any moment—as soon as the French example receded—by a barbarism ignorant of its own language or a pedantry uncertain of its own mind.

A civilized composer—'in the musical language of our own time, a civilized artist of the age of Pericles', said M. Koechlin with reference to Fauré's opera *Pénélope*.[1] And indeed it is impossible to discuss Fauré without considering that resemblance to Hellenic antiquity which in his day was more truly characteristic of French culture than at any other time since Chateaubriand observed it at the end of the eighteenth century. The highly sensitive but never exhibitionist art of Fauré merits the epithet of Hellenic to a degree all the greater because of the grounds on which he has sometimes been denied it; for the honour is withheld all the more jealously by those who themselves could never deserve it. M. Koechlin, on the other hand, had no doubts of Fauré's Hellenism; but his book, as it concerned many countries outside France, was unfortunate in its date. It was published in 1927, so that in England it encountered the deadweight of all that was most Bœotian in our established musical prejudices. The spokesmen of our public opinion were for the most part so absorbed in celebrating the centenaries of Beethoven and Schubert that they were unwilling to allow a

[1] Charles Koechlin, *Gabriel Fauré*, p. 142.

place, elsewhere than on the mere periphery of art, to any music that had developed independently of the German tradition. 'Why drag in the Hellenes?' asked one reviewer; and went on to scout the idea that Fauré could be anything but an 'exquisite Parisian'—an inevitably derogatory shade being implicit in the phrase. M. Koechlin had in fact anticipated this criticism, both in its substance and in its choice of words: '*exquisite*', he remarked, 'is a word very much weakened in meaning.'[1] It is one particularly appropriate to Fauré's music, but only if taken in its proper sense, as implying a supreme quality, not a limitation.

To a lesser extent the situation was similar in France itself. M. Koechlin noted the existence among his own countrymen of a discerning élite, a 'Fauréan freemasonry', but had to admit that its influence was counteracted, not only by the uncultured masses, but 'especially—and this is more serious—by those devotees whose culture derives principally from the art of Beethoven and his successors'.[2]

A great deal of Fauré's significance depends upon his having shown, by the force of his own unanswerable example, that the way of writing music which German composers had continued and developed from Beethoven was not the only way—and he showed it more effectively than many others because, unlike the generality of French composers, he was perfectly able to meet the Germans on their own ground: I mean, in those departments of music which they themselves favoured, notably the lyric for voice and pianoforte and the chamber ensemble. But for this very reason the heralds of German musical hegemony find themselves obliged to deny the value of precisely those qualities which characterize Fauré's distinctive excellence.

His music is, for instance, so transparent that the lovers of the turgid have no option but to accuse him of a lack of profundity. This charge comes with particular readiness to those who in various other connexions are desirous of perpetuating the legend

[1] *Op. cit.*, p. 22.

[2] *Op. cit.*, p. 197. I apologize for the inadequacy of 'devotees' as a translation of *mélomanes*

of French frivolity, and who will therefore assume without further proof that so typical a French thinker as Voltaire was more shallow than, say, Fichte, because his writings are so much more transparent; ignoring entirely the fact that Fichte was at least as often *mistaken* as Voltaire, and not only as often, but with regard to the same matters. To this day one may hear Fauré described disparagingly as 'a drawing-room composer', 'charming but unsubstantial' and the like; mainly, no doubt, by people who know only a selection of his easier songs, do not suspect the existence of more than three or four of his ten full-length chamber works, and have never heard of *Pénélope*. Even so their error is culpable enough, for it is as though they should assume a vessel to be shallow because they can see the bottom of it. It is a well-known fact in physics that, if the bottom of a liquid can be seen, the depth appears less than it really is; but, to continue the physical analogy, it should be equally well known that the transparency, and therefore the apparent shallowness, is principally due to absence of impurities.

I am perhaps falling into the very error I describe when I add that Fauré's limpidity is sometimes deceptive as to his real intellectual depth. But I make the remark in order to clear up another and a similar misunderstanding; the word 'intellectual' being commonly used by German or German-inspired critics in as misleading a manner as the word 'profound'. They use it to denote sheer ingenuity, rather than mental grasp of an artistic design and of its parts in relation to the whole. That is the only sense I can discover, for example, in a verdict of Adolf Weissmann (*The Problems of Modern Music*) upon Tchaikovsky: 'He scarcely knows the meaning of intellectual construction.' That is to say, he does not exhaust the permutations and combinations of his material for the mere sake of exhausting them; but it has always seemed to me that to keep one's ingenuity thus in subordination to one's judgment is evidence rather of intellectual strength than otherwise. There is something of a parallel here with the architectural criticism of Ruskin, a great part of which resolves itself into a close concern with sculptural detail. Ruskin, indeed, explicitly disavowed any interest in 'line' and 'proportion of masses' as such, and found his satisfaction all the more on that account in Gothic architecture; but his complete misconception both of the art of antiquity and of the classical revival is equalled only by the incomprehension of such critics as Weissmann for the art of Fauré, whom indeed they hardly mention.[1] He is of course too classical for them; by which I mean, especially, that one of his capital qualities was a very sound sense of the proportion between outline and detail. At a time when—to pursue for a moment the comparison with architecture—most German composition resembled an edifice very solidly built of absolutely undistinguished materials and devoid of æsthetic direction, while on the other hand some of the Russians' work was like a building made of rare stone imperfectly quarried and impermanently put together, Fauré displayed a greater artistic probity than either. The result of his procedures is moreover that a single striking detail in his work may be studied with less disturbance of one's focus upon the whole, because it bears a well-thought-out relation to the general proportions. I hope that while my own comments may centre frequently upon such highly charged *moments* of Fauré's works, I shall thus not lose sight of their structural unity.

Not only does Fauré never allow structural mechanics to run away with him; he does not, furthermore, allow emotion to overflow. For him the cultivation of excited states of mind, and the display of feelings for their own sake, was as irrelevant to the artistic purpose as was the spectacle of bloodshed for the writers of classical tragedy. As a critic of his own nation remarked:

> Out of a sensitive regard for beauty and dignity of sound, he moderates the force of his lyric transports and moulds them into graceful form.[2]

[1] Even Abert's *Illustriertes Musiklexicon* allots him no more than a bare biographical entry, of considerably smaller dimensions than those reserved for either Saint-Saëns or Ravel.

[2] 'Avec un pudique souci d'eurythmie et de noblesse, il modère l'élan passionné de son lyrisme; il l'assouplit dans la grâce.' J. Saint-Jean (*i.e.* J. de Marliave) in *La Nouvelle Revue*, Vol. xiii, p. 263 (1910).

He had, that is to say, that respect for his art which will not descend to making an easy impression by means of the *ugly* and the *undignified*; a Mozartian discretion which was once described to me in less sympathetic terms by a famous pianist, who said that Fauré's music was 'too damned polite'. Unsympathetic in a somewhat different direction are those romantically-minded people who consider him 'cold' or 'formally perfect but unemotional'—and who may usually be relied upon to make the same objection to Bach,[1] thus revealing their criticism for the unconscious compliment that it is. With Fauré the distinction between form and content does not survive the process of composition; for its survival would have been a confession of imperfect artistry. His aversion, in the true Hellenic succession, from what was amorphous and chaotic, is evidence that he possessed that supreme artistic quality, perfect command of his material. His attainment of this quality, so that his feelings do not burst their bounds but are resolved into form, thus showing that 'one may have a great deal to say and yet not be content to say it just anyhow', explains why he is an object of dislike to the romantic mentality which excuses its lack of artistic integrity by 'trusting that much will be forgiven to a warm heart'.[2]

As long as such a mentality reigned in the musical world, justice could hardly be done to a composer whose music does not vociferate, nor attempt to recall in its inflexions the accents of emotionally coloured speech, nor aim at giving its hearers 'an uncomfortable feeling inside'. Fauré's achievement is of a very different kind: the expressiveness of his work derives purely from its musical invention—what in another art would be called its *plastic* qualities—and owes nothing to outward signs of 'warmth' in performance. This equates him in music with the so-called 'Parnassians' of poetry, whose great service to their art was to remind us that 'the æsthetic emotion has an intellectual basis'[3]—that to rely upon a display of 'palpitations' in art

[1] As M. Koechlin found: *op. cit.*, p. 198.

[2] Jankélévitch, *Gabriel Fauré et ses mélodies*, p. 53.

[3] Julien Benda, *Belphégor*, p. 58. This is none the less true for being written by a thinker who misunderstood the real nature of music itself.

merely indicates an imperfect resolution of one's material—and explains why he was one of the earliest composers to rise to supreme heights subsequently to, and independently of, the romanticism whose bankruptcy was so painfully evident, for discerning minds, by the time he appeared on the musical scene.

CHAPTER II

MAINLY BIOGRAPHICAL

Gabriel-Urbain Fauré was born on 12th[1] May 1845 in the little town of Pamiers, which lies in the department of Ariège, not far from Foix and Carcassonne—the eastern-Pyrenean country of the ancient Albigensian culture and other historic memories He belongs to the company of those musicians whose talent was not, as far as we know, hereditary; for his ancestors had for some generations carried on the trade of butcher. Many years later, when Alfred Bruneau succeeded to Fauré's place in the Institut de France, and delivered the traditionally requisite memorial speech upon his predecessor, he referred to the composer's grandfather and great-grandfather with a certain delightful grandiloquence as 'industrious tradesmen who made a prosaic but profitable contribution to the nourishment of their fellow-citizens'.[2] The father, however, Toussaint-Honoré Fauré, abandoned the family business for the teaching profession, and at the time of his marriage in 1829 was a village schoolmaster at a little place called Gailhac-Toulza in the same department. His salary there was 300 francs per year, which even allowing for modern devaluation of money in general (and not merely that of the French franc in foreign exchange) was an income only practicable in village life where a great deal of one's sustenance came by supplementary payments in kind. But he was confident enough to marry, at the age of nineteen, a wife no richer than himself: Marie-Antoinette-Hélène Lalène, daughter of a retired army officer, whose retirement had

[1] Not 13th, as stated in many musical dictionaries: an error due apparently to someone who copied an entry of that date from the Pamiers civil register without noticing that the child is there described as having been 'born *yesterday*'.

[2] 'Des commerçants actifs qui contribuèrent prosaïquement, mais utilement, à l'alimentation de leurs concitoyens.' (Bruneau, *La Vie et les œuvres de Gabriel Fauré*, 1925, p. 8.)

apparently been hastened by his own desire—in order to avoid marrying his colonel's daughter—but whose family had some pretensions to nobility and had resumed, after the Revolutionary and Napoleonic troubles were over, the full name 'de Lalène-Laprade'.

In 1839 Toussaint-Honoré Fauré was appointed assistant inspector of elementary schools at Pamiers, where his younger children were born, Gabriel being the last of six. It is not surprising, in view of the family circumstances, that he was almost 'an unwanted child'. Baptized by the names of Gabriel after his grandfather and Urbain after a maternal uncle, he was put out to nurse at a neighbouring village, Verniolles, where he remained for the first four years of his life, until in 1849 he returned to the domestic circle, now established at Montgauzy near Foix, where his father had just been promoted to the post of director of the teachers' training college (*École normale*). Evidently he was not brought up in an atmosphere of intimate tenderness, either before or after the move to Montgauzy, where he had to live in a household rather preoccupied with the economic budget and in the company of a sister and four brothers, one of whom is reported to have been given to practical jokes such as throwing a plateful of spinach in his face in order to wake him from his meditations. All this must have encouraged a reticence, a capacity to find his satisfaction in his own inner consciousness, which was doubtless native to his character and which rendered him all his life reluctant to be effusive or to make easy confidences.[1]

Montgauzy had for many centuries been a place of pilgrimage, and the chapel—part of the old convent buildings out of whose ruins the *École normale* had arisen—was still in use. The child Gabriel Fauré spent a good deal of his time there, much to the satisfaction of his foster-mother, who had visions of his becoming a bishop. But, though he was in fact once discovered burying a grasshopper in the churchyard with full ecclesiastical rites, the main attraction of the place was evidently its music. The chapel had only a harmonium, but he was often to be found listening

1 'Even as a child', he once wrote, 'my parents tell me I was very thoughtful and silent.' (P. Fauré-Fremiet, *Gabriel Fauré*, p. 26.)

FAURÉ'S MOTHER

FAURÉ'S FATHER—TOUSSAINT FAURÉ

to it and in time tried his own hands at it; thus he took, independently, his first step towards musicianship and came to spend more and more time in his tentative improvisations. It happened that an old blind lady, who frequented the chapel for her private prayers, heard him play and was struck by his promise. She conferred with his parents on what she had heard; this boy undoubtedly had gifts, and it was plain he should be sent to the Niedermeyer school.

Louis Niedermeyer, a Swiss from Nyon on the Lake of Geneva, was in 1854 a person of considerable distinction in Parisian musical life. Himself a composer in a small way—famous in his time for a setting of Lamartine's well-known poem *Le Lac*, which is said to have caused Lamartine himself some annoyance, on perhaps justifiable grounds[1]—he deserves an honourable name in musical history for his work as an educator. In a way his career reads like an anticipation of that of Charles Bordes half a century later. He began in 1843 by founding a 'Société de musique vocale religieuse et classique' for the performance of those sixteenth- and seventeenth-century works which were as generally forgotten at the time in France as elsewhere; and managed to interest an influential section of Parisian society in the performances. The society lasted only a few years, but left its mark in eleven published volumes of its repertory.

Niedermeyer next turned his attention to the standard of music in the churches, where, as Fauré himself remarked in later years, 'though bad music is every day becoming more and more the exception, about the middle of last century it was almost the general rule'.[2] He therefore decided to open a school for the training of organists, choirmasters and teachers of music; and, availing himself of the already existing but moribund school previously founded by Choron, he again canvassed the support of prominent social figures and even that of the State, so that in 1853 he was able to establish the 'École de musique religieuse

[1] See p. 60. He also wrote for the stage.

[2] For this and for most of my account of Niedermeyer I have drawn on Fauré's own *Souvenirs* in the *Revue musicale*, October 1922.

et classique' which came to be called familiarly by his name. He ran it as a boarding-school with a musical bias; the usual literary subjects of a school curriculum were taught there as well as music. On the musical side the pupils learned the pianoforte and the organ, harmony and counterpoint, all with a view primarily to the career of a church musician or a teacher of music; and in particular they were given a thorough grounding in Gregorian plainchant and how to accompany it. No doubt the methods employed in this branch of study left something to be desired from the point of view of the Solesmes and other recent researches; but it was at least a good beginning to be able to learn plainchant in a form which avoided, at any rate, the violences habitually practised upon it before Niedermeyer's time in order to fit it to the Procrustean bed of modern major and minor tonality.

To this school, then, Gabriel Fauré was sent at the age of nine. His father, following the old lady's advice, had written to the director, who was fortunately about to visit Foix in the course of a concert-tour, and undertook to come and test the child's power for himself. The original idea was to apply for a scholarship which would have reduced the fees payable by about one-half; but the impression that young Gabriel made on Niedermeyer, enhanced by the support of M. de Saubiac, parliamentary deputy for the department, who had also been enlisted in his cause, was such that he consented to waive the fees altogether. Toussaint Fauré, still not a wealthy man, was thus relieved of anxiety concerning his youngest son, who was assured of a sound education and a reasonably secure career as organist at the end of it. The buildings, situated in what is now Rue Fromentin, off the Boulevard de Clichy, were not remarkable for comfort, and the conditions of work were such that a dozen or more pupils would be accommodated in the same room, each playing a different piece on a different piano; but this did no more than intensify the capacity for abstraction which is the only resource of a sensitive child in the atmosphere of a boarding-school. And Fauré himself always spoke of the place with the most grateful remembrance.

Niedermeyer died in 1861. The surviving professor of harmony was Dietsch, choirmaster at the Madeleine and conductor at the Paris Opéra: the same who had once been commissioned by an Opéra director to write a *Flying Dutchman* on a libretto translated from Wagner's own. But a year earlier another professor of the piano had joined the staff—Camille Saint-Saëns, a young man only ten years older than Fauré himself, but already launched on his brilliant career as concert pianist and composer. This was the beginning of a lifelong friendship. Saint-Saëns encouraged Fauré and eased his way throughout his career, and would speak of the early relation between them as one of the things he himself had most reason to remember with pride. He did not limit himself to the statutory piano lessons; he would play for the students, outside the regular class hours, music which they had few opportunities of hearing elsewhere—Wagner, for example[1]; and he examined their own essays in composition with an attentiveness which, as Fauré remarked, would have done honour to genuine masterpieces. It is difficult to overvalue the benefits thus conferred by a teacher whose excessive fondness for Liszt, even, was compensated by his active propaganda for Bach, and whose taste for other forms of music besides the opera and the *Prix-de-Rome* cantata increased the appropriateness of the Niedermeyer education for one whose own inclinations were all towards the less spectacular forms.

Fauré's student-years produced, as might be supposed, a crop of anecdotes. One of them assumes a somewhat familiar pattern: he and his schoolfellow Eugène Gigout were taking a Sunday walk and, surveying Paris and its churches from the top of the Montmartre hill, were moved to declare that they would one day be organists, Fauré at the Madeleine and Gigout at Saint-Augustin—both of which prophecies came true. Another

[1] Koechlin, *op. cit.*, p. 8, based on a memorial article by Fauré in the *Revue musicale* for February 1922. Of course in the 1860s this would necessarily mean the earlier Wagner, up to and including *Lohengrin*; but it may have been partly because of this youthful initiation that Fauré did not, like so many others, lose his head when the serious craze for Wagner came twenty years later.

relates that the same two inseparable companions, having spent their savings on seats at the Théâtre-Lyrique for a performance of Gounod's *Faust*—in those days a novelty, regarded with some suspicion by the pundits—were obliged to wander about the city in the small hours until half-past five, when they were able to snatch a little uncertain slumber in a church while waiting for the school gates to open.

Fauré completed his studies in 1865 with numerous distinctions, and early in the next year obtained his first professional post, that of organist in the church of Saint-Sauveur at Rennes in Brittany. There he appears to have shown what Harvey Grace called 'the traditional organist's impatience of the pulpit',[1] for the priest in charge complained that he could be seen smoking cigarettes in the porch during sermons. After some four years he was found guilty of an even more serious offence: having spent Saturday night at a ball in the town, he appeared the next morning in his organ-loft still wearing evening dress. This was too much for the authorities, and he was asked to leave. He found another appointment, this time in Paris, at Notre-Dame de Clignancourt on the northern outskirts; leaving it soon afterwards for Saint-Honoré d'Eylau and later assisting Widor at Saint-Sulpice.[2] He also took Saint-Saëns's place at the Madeleine on the numerous occasions when that versatile and much-travelling musician was called out of Paris by his concert engagements. The two had indeed not lost contact by absence; Saint-Saëns had helped to bring him out as a composer while he was at Rennes, by inviting him to deputize as accompanist to a singer, Mme. Miolan-Carvalho, whose concert tours took her into Brittany, and suggesting that she should reward her young colleague by including one of his songs in her programme. Fauré presented her with *Le Papillon et la fleur*, with which she made a great success.

[1] Grace, *The Organ Works of Bach*.

[2] In the larger Parisian churches it is customary to appoint, besides the organist proper, an assistant who is not merely a deputy but is more specially concerned with the training of the choir, for which reason he is called *maître de chapelle*.

He had returned to the École Niedermeyer as a member of the teaching staff[1]; but before this there had come the Franco-Prussian war, when he enlisted in a regiment of light infantry and saw some active service until the Prussian victory, and the ensuing Communard disturbances, left him no option but to escape to Rambouillet with a forged passport, there to await the establishment of the Third Republic. Thenceforward his career, though slow and not very well paid, was steady and promising; and he had reason to feel firmly established when in 1877 Saint-Saëns, finding his post at the Madeleine finally incompatible with his travels, resigned it in favour of his *maître de chapelle*, Théodore Dubois, whose own functions were then taken over by Fauré. Towards the end of the same year Saint-Saëns took him to Weimar, where *Samson et Dalila* was to receive its first performance by the good offices of Liszt; and he visited Germany again in the two years following, to hear the first two parts of Wagner's *Ring* at Cologne and the whole cycle at Munich.[2] He had been introduced by Saint-Saëns to Liszt at Weimar and improved the occasion by offering to the old master his *Ballade* (Op. 19) in its original form as a pianoforte solo. But Liszt never played it; after trying a page or two he returned it with the curious comment that it was *too difficult*.

However, another composition of Fauré's had slightly better fortune. A Sonata in A major for violin and pianoforte, which he had written in 1876, was accepted for performance at the Trocadéro in the concerts of the 1878 Exhibition, where the composer himself played it with the violinist Maurin[3].

[1] One of his earliest pupils was André Messager, the comic-opera composer and first conductor of Debussy's *Pelléas*.

[2] This was evidently more of a financial strain to him than might be supposed; and even half a dozen years later he was able to visit Bayreuth, in company with Messager, only because the expenses had been subscribed by a group of his friends, headed by Mme. Baugnies.

[3] He tried his hand after this at a violin Concerto, but never published it; according to Octave Séré (*Musiciens français d'aujourd'hui*, p. 185) it was performed in 1879, but Philippe Fauré-Fremiet (*op. cit.*, p. 86) says that only the first movement was ever written.

Saint-Saëns welcomed it with an enthusiastic article in the *Journal de musique.* It was even printed—but by the firm of Breitkopf & Härtel, at Leipzig; no Parisian publisher would have anything to do with it, and even Breitkopfs took it only on condition that Fauré should receive neither initial payment nor royalties. When he found a regular publisher in Paris (Hamelle) the terms were not much better: he had to sell his songs outright for an average of fifty francs each, and he was paid nothing for either of the two pianoforte Quartets written in 1879 and 1886. The advantage of the Breitkopf publication was purely from the point of view of fame; and this was the ground on which he was advised to agree to the contract, by his friend Camille Clerc, a cultured man of business to whose mediation it was indeed due that the Leipzig firm had made any offer at all. He and his wife were among Fauré's closest friends in Paris; the Sonata had been written in his house, and tried out progressively with another of his visitors, the famous Belgian violinist Léonard—to whom the first Quartet was afterwards dedicated. The friendship with Mme. Clerc was kept up until her death, five years before Fauré's own; but Clerc himself died prematurely in 1880—not, however, without having the satisfaction of knowing that his hospitable house had been not only the cradle of Fauré's first great compositions, but a refuge for him upon his disappointment in love.

For, towards the end of 1877, his engagement to Marianne Viardot had been broken off. This lady was the younger daughter of a distinguished family; her mother was Pauline Viardot-Garcia, sister of the celebrated singer Maria Malibran and of the singing-teacher Manuel Garcia, and herself vocally gifted in no small degree, having been hailed in verse by Alfred de Musset on her first appearance at the same time as the tragic actress Rachel. Marianne and her sister both sang also, and their brother Paul played the violin. (The A major Sonata is dedicated to him.) The Viardot household exuded an atmosphere not only of music but of literature, for it received as a constant visitor the Russian novelist Turgenev, whom all the family called *parrain*. Fauré had been introduced there by Saint-Saëns in 1872, and soon became a regular participator in the charades and literary parties which were a feature of the house. He paid his addresses to Marianne for more than four years; she accepted him just before going away for a summer vacation, and while they were parted he wrote her thirty-five letters in three weeks. But the engagement was broken almost immediately after this very summer, it is not known exactly why. There is little doubt that Marianne Viardot did not return his affection in the same degree as it was offered; perhaps this reserved, undemonstrative man did not appear a convincing lover to one of her bohemian upbringing. It has also been suggested that Pauline Viardot was too anxious to make an operatic composer of him: an idea fortified by a remark made by Fauré himself: 'Perhaps the break was not a bad thing for me; the Viardot family might have deflected me from my proper path.'[1] And one thinks of his maternal grandfather and the grounds for that officer's early retirement. Finally—although we know that he took years to recover from the blow, and kept to the end of his life the letters which Marianne had returned to him[2]—is it possible that Fauré himself wanted a home-making rather than a 'bohemian' marriage?

At all events, when he did get married, in 1883, it was to a very different person. Marie Fremiet was the daughter of a celebrated sculptor; but in her, and perhaps in her family in general, the artistic ancestry did not run true to type. M. Koechlin describes her as 'essentially the home-making kind of wife'[3], and the marriage seems to have been a pattern of the traditionally French family alliance. Fauré's relations with his wife give, from all accounts, the impression of having been reverent rather than tender; a typical example of his solicitude is provided by his apprehension in 1920 that she might not view his *grand cordon* of the Legion of Honour with unmixed joy,

[1] P. Fauré-Fremiet, *op. cit.*, p. 43.

[2] They were printed, with an introduction by C. Bellaigue, in the *Revue des Deux Mondes* for 15th August 1928.

[3] 'Essentiellement une femme d'intérieur', *op. cit.*, p. 16.

because her father had never had it.[1] The slender evidence available as to her character rather reminds us of Barrett Wendell's description of the ideal French married woman: 'she is not only a good wife, but remains what she was as a girl—a model daughter, deeply attached to her own family.'[2] And her importance was for Fauré's family life, not for his professional career. She did some decorative painting, which supplemented his very moderate income from private lessons and his post at the Madeleine; but otherwise her attention was absorbed by domestic matters, and she never accompanied Fauré on his various musical journeyings. They had two sons; the elder, Emmanuel, inherited some of the Fremiet sculptural gift[3] and has attained some celebrity as a biologist, while Philippe, the younger, has devoted himself mainly to literature—he wrote a carefully documented life of his father (on which I have drawn extensively for these pages) and another of his grandfather Emmanuel Fremiet, and is furthermore the author of a play, *Le Souffle du désordre*, besides philosophical essays.

As a composer Fauré was acquiring a reputation by slow degrees. A Symphony by him (which, like nearly all his other youthful efforts in the larger orchestral forms, he afterwards suppressed) was played in 1885 at the Colonne concerts, and repeated the same year under Vincent d'Indy's direction at the concerts organized by Peter Benoit at Antwerp. A little later he came to the notice of the Parisian theatre-public by the incidental music he provided at the Odéon for Alexandre Dumas's play *Caligula* and for Edmond Haraucourt's Shakespearean adaptation, *Shylock*. It is true that his first attempt to obtain a professorship of composition at the Conservatoire was indignantly repulsed by Ambroise Thomas, the director, outraged at the idea of such an application from one who was neither a Rome scholar nor even a Conservatoire pupil; if

[1] P. Fauré-Fremiet, *op. cit.*, p. 84.

[2] *La France d'aujourd'hui*, p. 142. I am re-translating from the French version of Wendell's book and cannot therefore be certain of quoting his exact words.

[3] He executed, among other things, a bust of his father.

Fauré were appointed, he said, then he, Thomas, would resign.[1] But his songs, his piano pieces—the Chopinesque early *Nocturnes* and *Impromptus* and the *Barcarolles* for which he had a special predilection—and his chamber music appeared in concert programmes with a certain frequency, notably in those of the Société Nationale.

The 'Société nationale de musique française', to give it its full and significant name, was one of numerous determined efforts made under the Third Republic to show that French musicians had something to say for themselves elsewhere than in the opera. It had been founded in 1871 by the combined efforts of Saint-Saëns and a Conservatoire professor of singing named Romain Bussine, and its motto was *Ars Gallica.* The committee included Franck, Lalo, Dubois, Ernest Guiraud and Fauré himself; and the first secretary was Alexis de Castillon, the gifted but unlucky Franck pupil, who drew up the Society's rules but survived its foundation barely two years. The programmes of its concerts consisted at first of French works exclusively; and after a time they developed a noticeable bias towards the music of the Franckist school, so that the Society was accused of being 'almost a *succursale* of the Schola Cantorum'.[2] But this was rather after the death of Franck, and for some years the Society did Fauré good service.

To this period also belongs one of the highest peaks touched by his genius as a composer. His father, who had finally retired from the educational service and spent his last years at Toulouse, died in 1885; and this fortified the invitation, always open to a church musician, to write a Requiem Mass. Fauré's Requiem occupied him during the year following; and by the time it was ready to be used for the first time at a Madeleine service (in 1888) his mother was dead also.

This was the heaviest-burdened period of his life. He had not been able to be present for his father's last hours, for at that very time his wife's health was causing him anxiety, and he had to arrange for her to take a cure at a health resort. His financial position was no easier: to maintain his income he was

[1] Koechlin, *op. cit.*, p. 17.

[2] Koechlin, *op. cit.*, p. 36.

still obliged to travel several times a week into the Paris suburbs, where he gave private lessons, and his compositions brought him fame (including the Chartier prize, awarded him by the Académie des Beaux-Arts for his chamber music) but little money. His various worries combined to aggravate an old tendency towards neuralgic pains, so that he was now scarcely a day without violent headaches and dizziness.

At this juncture the situation was relieved by the Princesse Edmond de Polignac (Princesse de Scey-Montbéliard as she was then), the American lady[1] whom so many artists of Fauré's and subsequent generations have cause to remember with gratitude. She made it possible for him and some of his friends to take a holiday at Venice, a place which had always attracted him, as was attested by his fondness for writing in the barcarolle rhythm, but which he had hitherto been obliged to enjoy by report only. This brief but precious intermission was the saving of him: his health recovered, his preoccupations were dispelled by contact with the fascinating and improbable city, and he found the opportunity to develop a vein in composition which, represented hitherto by two songs (notably the unsurpassed *Clair de lune*) was to issue in two further series of masterpieces —the setting of poems by Verlaine. In Venice he planned a group of five songs to Verlaine's words, which he sent to his friend Mme. Baugnies with, at first, half a mind that she should keep them to sing on private occasions only; then, deciding to let them see the light after all, he published them with a dedication to the Princesse. It seemed to him at the time that these were all the Verlaine that could serve his turn, but within a year he had found the material for a cycle of nine more, *La Bonne Chanson* (1891), one of the high-water marks of his art. Between the two he planned another chamber work, a pianoforte Quintet for Eugène Ysaÿe; but he was not satisfied with the shape it took, and it did not appear until 1906.

The dark hour before the Venetian holiday was evidently he prelude to a dawn; substantial recognition was beginning

[1] She was a Miss Singer, of the family of the well-known sewing-machine manufacturer.

to come to Fauré. He succeeded Guiraud in 1892 as inspector of music in state-aided provincial conservatoires, which involved a good deal of travelling but relieved him from dependence upon private lessons, especially when four years later, being already over fifty years old, he at last obtained a professorship of composition[1] at the Conservatoire of Paris and the chief organist's post at the Madeleine. The immediate cause of these various moves was the death of Ambroise Thomas, the director who had hitherto kept him out. The Ministry of Public Instruction decided that in future it would not appoint a director for life; which gave mortal offence to Massenet, who had hoped to succeed Thomas but had no intention of accepting the post on less favourable terms than his. Théodore Dubois was appointed instead, and Massenet, thoroughly piqued, left the Conservatoire altogether; the chair which he resigned was given to Fauré, who also stepped into the place vacated by Dubois at the Madeleine organ.

The change of professor made a considerable difference to the Conservatoire class; Massenet had been an active and voluble adviser, Fauré was described by one of his pupils as 'less a teacher than a guide'[2], and his influence evidently derived, even more than his predecessor's, from the attraction exercised by his own compositions. Neither of them was an adept in the purely academic studies of counterpoint and fugue, and both were fortunate in being able to rely, in compensation of this deficiency, upon their colleague, the excellent polyphonist André Gédalge. But whereas Massenet, as might be expected, fitted in perfectly with the traditional bias of the Conservatoire towards theatrical works, Fauré reserved his best attention for chamber music; orchestration counted for as little in his teaching as in his own practice, and for the dramatic cantata required in *Prix de Rome* competitions he had so little use that his class turned out very few Rome scholars. What it did produce, however, was a major proportion of the outstanding names in French composition of

[1] To which the salary attached was the not very princely sum of 3,000 francs a year.

[2] Quoted by Bruneau, *op. cit.*, pp. 26-7.

the present century; Louis Aubert, Nadia Boulanger, Roger-Ducasse, Grovlez, Koechlin, Ravel, Florent Schmitt and Vuillermoz were all his pupils, and this list is only a selection. Its one rival is the following of Franck, represented especially by the pupils of Vincent d'Indy at the Schola Cantorum; apart from these, one is likely to find that even such composers as Dukas and Honegger, who did not sit officially at Fauré's feet, came nevertheless under his influence.

Invitations to compose for special occasions were moreover coming in from various sides. One was in 1898 from the Prince of Wales Theatre in London, where incidental music was required for the production of Maeterlinck's *Pelléas et Mélisande*, to be staged with Martin-Harvey and Mrs. Patrick Campbell in the principal parts. For this purpose Fauré, besides writing fresh pieces (including a song with English words for Mélisande) incorporated a slightly older one, the *Sicilienne* for violoncello, and left the whole, as was his wont, to be orchestrated by another hand: in this case that of his pupil Charles Koechlin—but though he had delegated the scoring, he came himself to London to conduct the little theatre orchestra.[1] Two years later came a commission on a larger scale. The town of Béziers in Languedoc (a little to the east of Fauré's own native district), possessing an open-air amphitheatre reconstructed from the antique type, was fortunate also in a wealthy patron of the arts, named Castelbon de Beauxhostes, who for some years subsidized a series of dramatic productions on this stage, modelled on classical tragedy. The idea had apparently been suggested to him by Saint-Saëns, who himself wrote the music for some of the productions (*Déjanire* in 1898, *Parysatis* in 1902); and for the festival of 1900 the promoters fixed upon the legend of Prometheus. The text, by Jean Lorrain and Ferdinand Hérold, treated of Prometheus's stealing of the fire from heaven and of

[1] This, however, was not his first nor his only visit to England; the Princesse Edmond de Polignac records that in 1896 he gave a concert in London at the invitation of Mr. Frank Schuster, and Sir Adrian Boult tells me that he saw him more than once at the house of the same host in the early years of this century.

FAURÉ AT THE AGE OF 18

ME. FAURÉ AT THE TIME OF
HER MARRIAGE

the revenge taken by the gods, who neutralized the gift by sending Pandora to earth with her box, in which were all human sufferings; and it was planned to be partly spoken and partly sung. The protagonists, Prometheus and Pandora, were to have purely speaking parts; the divine personages, Hephæstus and the rest, were to be played by singers; and there were two choruses, one of Prometheus's human companions and the other of the Ocean Nymphs, his sympathizers in misfortune. An orchestra was provided, somewhat originally constituted, for it consisted of a local orchestral society (called 'la Lyre bitterroise'[1]) together with a dozen harps and the military band of a regiment of engineers. (The orchestration in its final form was again not Fauré's own; it was entrusted to Eustace, the bandmaster of this regiment.) Fauré undertook the job in one of the hottest summers on record and—in addition to the dissatisfied feelings normally deriving from work written to order—wondered how he was going to avoid the resemblances to Wagner which the poem seemed to invite; the warning of Gaia, not to steal the fire, at once suggested Erda in the *Rheingold*, the Ocean Nymphs bore a certain resemblance to Rhine-maidens, and the conclusion—in which humanity hails the shining example of Prometheus amid the ills now falling to its lot—offered a parallel to the closing scene in *Götterdämmerung*. The work brought its inevitable discouragements; the local performers were as helpful as he could wish, as also were De Max and Cora Laparcerie, the Parisian stars brought in to take the two leading parts; but the tenor chosen at first to play Kratos threw up his part a week before the production was due, because Fauré would not meet his demands in the matter of a high C and similar operatic tricks (his successor, Fonteix, was fortunately more amenable), and even Vallier, who played Hephæstus after distinguishing himself as King Mark at the Paris Opéra, never quite reconciled himself to not ending one of his arias with a high F. There were compensations of another kind; Fauré wrote with amuse-

[1] *I.e.* of Béziers; the French language is particularly rich in these half-recognizable territorial adjectives of the type of our 'Mancunian' or 'Salopian'.

ment to his wife that at last he knew what fame was, for he had just seen the latest creation in boots named after him in a Béziers shop-window.[1] But the worst alarm came two days before production date, when Béziers was swept by a terrific thunderstorm; as Pierre Lalo said, reviewing the festival in *Le Temps*[2], it was as though Zeus had once more visited his spite upon Prometheus. The scenery was almost ruined, and by a rueful coincidence (so Fauré wrote to his wife) the lightning had struck the very place on the stage where Prometheus was to steal the fire. However, by dint of great labour the stage-set was put to rights; the harps fortunately escaped damage; and the weather recovered magnificently, so that when Saint-Saëns opened the proceedings by conducting a prelude he had written for the occasion (making prominent use of the formidable array of harps) it was a glorious summer evening. Fauré was able to conduct *Prométhée* under ideal conditions; the amphitheatre, large enough to seat twenty thousand people, was nevertheless acoustically so good that no sound was lost; and at the moment of Prometheus's chaining to the rock the stage was irradiated by a rich sunset which acted as an unspoken comment of crowning appropriateness.

Prométhée was repeated the next year in the same setting, confirming its original impression; but subsequent attempts to transplant it were not successful. In 1907 it was revived at a benefit performance to raise money for the victims of a flood; the place was the Paris Hippodrome, where both the lighting and the acoustics appear to have been thoroughly unsuitable. The promoter, Pedro Gailhard, transferred it by a desperate effort to the Opéra, making use of the scenery normally belonging to Brünnhilde's rock in *The Valkyrie*, and there the effect was better. But besides the scoring, the whole conception of *Prométhée* belongs essentially to the outdoor theatre and the clear southern climate, and its leisurely length fits it rather for festival conditions than for the hurried life of a metropolitan theatrical world.

[1] P. Fauré-Fremiet, *op. cit.*, p. 57. ('Dernière création; les élégantes Gabriel Fauré!')
[2] Issue of 5th October 1900.

There was no doubt that the name of Fauré, now in his later fifties, had come to carry weight. The celebrated journalist Gaston Calmette invited him in 1903 to write musical criticism for the *Figaro*, where he concerned himself more particularly with first performances and notable revivals, especially of theatrical works, with the result that we have from him, among other things, original impressions of Puccini's *Tosca* and *Madam Butterfly* as well as some penetrating remarks upon the operas of Gluck and Mozart. (It is noteworthy that there was no intransigence towards the theatre in this composer, who reached the age of sixty before embarking upon a full-length stage work of his own.) Then, in 1905, came another upheaval in the affairs of the Paris Conservatoire: Dubois resigned, and Fauré—to most people's surprise, for he was not a member of the Institut, and was well known to have received his education at the École Niedermeyer, where the Conservatoire was regarded somewhat as a house of musical ill-fame—became director in his place.

This was much more than a routine official appointment; in fact it was part of a far-reaching scheme of reform, for Conservatoire policy had for some time been giving general dissatisfaction. As early as 1892 there had been a Commission to revise the curriculum, with Vincent d'Indy as one of its members, and this had encountered such opposition among the teaching staff that it was dissolved without reaching any conclusions. No doubt it was partly his disappointment at this abortive result that impelled d'Indy four years later to join with Bordes and Guilmant in the foundation of a new school, the Schola Cantorum, where emphasis was laid from the first on what had always been the older establishment's weakest side: the history as distinct from the practice of music. For the trouble with the Conservatoire was one of a familiar pattern: should it incline towards the type of the university or the technical college? The tradition of the place was all in the latter direction; it was primarily a school for executant musicians, the occupation of composer being envisaged as an executant one along with the rest. As Pierre Lalo remarked[1], the Conservatoire taught musicians

[1] In *Le Temps*, 22nd August 1905.

their craft but not their art; the position was the exact reverse of that sometimes obtaining nowadays in certain musical institutions, where a student may know a great deal about the historical development of the harpsichord as well as the pianoforte but be incapable of playing convincingly upon either. To quote further from Lalo's report, Conservatoire pupils were like what university students in literature would be if they were ignorant of anything beyond the novels and the plays of their own century. It was still possible, he observed, to find Rome scholars who knew nothing of Beethoven's symphonies.[1] And for the teachers of singing he reserved strictures which in our own time and place would undoubtedly have landed him in a court of law. They were all ex-theatre-singers, he said, and knew less of vocal music itself than even that would imply; only a few arias for competition purposes. One thinks of the various anecdotes current in musical literature concerning opera singers who were ignorant either of the plot or of anyone else's part in the operas they sang. Doubtless Lalo, writing as a friend of Fauré's, was exaggerating, or the situation had worsened in a short time; we can hardly suppose the description to have applied, for example, to Bussine. But the general scope of the complaints he was voicing is understandable enough: the aim of Conservatoire teaching was to produce prizewinners rather than cultured musicians. String players, for instance, were not encouraged to exercise themselves in music for chamber ensemble; a chamber-music class there was, but it was too infrequent and invested with too little importance.[2] And the lack of historical back-

[1] Of course his choice of an example represents a bias in another direction; I should not like to count the number of musical academies all over Europe in which it is still possible to take a degree while knowing nothing of the operas of Rameau—or the chamber music of Fauré!

[2] The professor in charge of this class wrote to *Le Temps* protesting that it met, and was well attended, three times a week. Lalo retorted that he must then blame no one but himself, and not the general Conservatoire policy, for the poor level of ensemble playing both among the students and outside. Which reads a little like a journalist's desire to score off an opponent; but it evidently had some foundation.

ground provided a notable illustration of the well-known fact that a teacher is liable to be unsympathetic towards the art of the future in proportion as he is unacquainted with that of the past. The hard fight for modern painting in England was due chiefly to the ignorance of all but a few with regard to any painting other than the school of Raphael and the school of Leighton; the incomprehension of modern music all over Europe, which was such a feature of the 1900 period, is traceable mainly to the prevalent myopia of those for whom the maturity of music dated from Beethoven. What wonder, then, that such incomprehension, already displayed by Ambroise Thomas towards Fauré himself, should have given rise to a *cause célèbre*—the case of Ravel.

In 1901 Maurice Ravel had obtained a second class in the *Prix de Rome* competition; the next two years he was not placed; and in 1905 he was not allowed to take the examination. This treatment of a man now thirty years of age and already known as the composer of *Jeux d'eau*, the Quartet and the *Shéhérazade* songs, was obviously sheer prejudice; and it was the resulting wave of protest which was the immediate cause of Dubois's resignation. The Under-Secretary for Fine Arts, Dujardin-Beaumetz, to whom under the Ministry of Public Instruction it fell to choose a successor, thus appointed Fauré as a deliberate measure of a revised policy; and the choice might be exceptionally and disconcertingly regarded as an argument in favour of petticoat influence in high places, for it was due largely to the advice of the Prime Minister's wife, Mme. Rouvier.[1] When Dujardin-Beaumetz presented the assembled staff and pupils with their new director, he went almost out of his way to state that a plan of reform had been determined; and Fauré was no sooner installed than he began to carry it out. Some of the vices complained of were too deeply rooted in the system to be attacked at once. Instrumental solo teaching, for example, had still to be allowed to confine itself to exclusively virtuoso work drawn from the music of a single period[2], and even with the singing

[1] P. Fauré-Fremiet, *op cit.*, p. 67. M. Cortot assures me that this is the lady in question, not the Mme. Roujon mentioned by M. Koechlin (*op. cit.*, p. 34, n.).

[2] Koechlin, *op. cit.*, p. 32, n. This situation, however, was not

classes he could hardly do more than remind them of the existence of classical cantatas and *Lieder* as well as their inevitable concert arias. But he took decisive steps to ensure that musical education, in a broad sense, should henceforth not be neglected for the sake of purely technical instruction. On whom was this additional responsibility to rest? The professors of composition already had their attention fully absorbed by counterpoint, constructional form and the like; but there was at any rate one teacher on the staff, of whose services a more profitable use could be made—Bourgault-Ducoudray, the great authority on ancient music and folksong, who had a class in the history of music. Here I will leave Pierre Lalo, in *Le Temps*, to give his own account of the matter:

> M. Bourgault-Ducoudray's course has hitherto, unfortunately, been optional; and moreover such a course, to be effective in demonstration, must necessarily be illustrated with examples. But the other professors, to whose good will one would have to apply for this purpose, are not very willing to lend their pupils to his class. . . . Henceforth M. Bourgault-Ducoudray's course is to be placed on a broader and firmer footing and to constitute an essential, regular and obligatory part of the teaching at the Conservatoire. Pupils in the harmony and composition classes are to be required to attend it on pain of dismissal. The instrumental and vocal classes are to furnish any performers needed to illustrate the lessons with examples. Thus, from medieval monody to the dramatic and symphonic music of our own time, all musical forms will be studied both historically and æsthetically.

---

unrelieved by glimpses of better things, and moreover it improved during Fauré's tenure of office; as is attested by the fact that his own *Fantaisie* for flute (Op. 79) and *Impromptu* for harp (Op. 86) were written as test pieces for the Conservatoire competitions in 1898 and 1904 respectively, and No. 5 of the *Pièces brèves* (Op. 84) as a sight-reading example, and that in 1919 his seventh Nocturne was prescribed for one of the pianoforte tests.

It will be noticed that Lalo writes of 'the harmony and composition classes'. Until the time of Fauré's directorship it was the second of these—which a pupil did not enter until the later years of his course—that concerned itself with counterpoint and fugue; so that one studied harmony for some years without being introduced to the polyphonic principle. Fauré attempted to remedy this by creating two new counterpoint classes, to be begun after the first year of harmony, leaving fugue to be dealt with as before by the professors of composition. This had the unfortunate effect of separating counterpoint and fugue from each other, and (to anticipate in time for a moment) Rabaud, the next director, added fugue to the new classes; this in its turn has been adversely criticized as isolating all polyphonic study from the official content of the composition classes, but the matter is outside the scope of the present work.

Moderate as Fauré's reforms were, he had not been in his post three months when an organized revolt broke out among the staff. We have Pierre Lalo's word for it[1] that the teachers of composition were least concerned in this. In any case the point chosen on which to fight was not any part of the reforms I have been describing, but a comparatively small matter: the formation of selection committees for the admission of students. Lalo implied in his account of the affair that the professors were jealous of losing their influence on these committees because hitherto they had taken care to select only their own private pupils, thus giving it to be understood that no one could hope for a place in the Conservatoire unless he had been a private pupil first. Remembering what Fauré's own salary was when he first joined the staff[2], one can sympathize with professors who plainly had to find *some* way of supplementing the income of their posts; but there was evidently a certain justification for Lalo's comment that the result of their policy was to bar from the Paris institution those very students of the provincial Conservatoires who might be regarded as having first claim upon its

[1] *Le Temps*, 17th October 1905.

[2] See p. 21, n. As director he received 12,000 francs a year; the rate of pay had not been altered since Cherubini's time.

benefits. However that may be, when the malcontent professors made their organized protest to the Under-Secretary, the latter replied that he saw no reason to modify anything in the plan of reform which he had announced and the director had organized, so that Fauré had not to fear any failure of support from above. Equally it remained true that there were still persons among his colleagues upon whose loyalty he could not rely, and his position was not such that he could dismiss them out of hand. What he did therefore was to put into positions, involving constant contact with these obstructionists, persons with whom from mere lack of sympathy they would find it impossible to work; and after a time they usually resigned. So many of these resignations were there that people began to say of Fauré—whom they had known as a kind-hearted, mild-mannered man—that he 'needed his daily cartload of victims, like Robespierre'.[1] A humorous magazine published a cartoon in which he was represented as interviewing, for a post at the Conservatoire, a man with the appearance of a racing tout; the implication being that with the disappearance of so many recognized professional musicians he would be reduced to drawing on such persons to replace them. The most sensational resignation of all was that of Théodore Dubois, who had remained on the *Conseil supérieur* as a professor emeritus, but left it in November 1905 stating publicly that he did so 'because M. Fauré was transforming the Conservatoire into a temple for the music of the future'. Philippe Fauré states, however[2], that the real reason for Dubois's resignation was the appointment of Pierre Lalo to the *Conseil*. A very piquant situation was thus created in that to Lalo himself fell the task of commenting on his departure for the benefit of the reading public.[3] Dubois's accusation, he said, was the exact reverse of the truth: 'all the reforms accomplished or planned by M. Dujardin-Beaumetz and M. Fauré have as their object to introduce or strengthen the study of older music.' What was Dubois complaining about? The new regulations for Bourgault-Ducoudray's class?

[1] P. Fauré-Fremiet, *op. cit.*, p. 68. [2] *Ibid.*

[3] In *Le Temps*, 21st November 1905.

> To bring the existence of Palestrina, or Monteverdi, or Schütz, or Rameau to the notice of students who were peacefully ignorant of any such matters in M. Dubois's time—is that what he calls 'making the Conservatoire into a temple for the music of the future'?

Or did he object to the arrangement whereby the insufficiency of the time hitherto devoted to counterpoint had been remedied by creating a new class on a wider basis for the invaluable Gédalge? This newspaper polemic seems to me to illustrate one fact very clearly: that Fauré's very real modern sympathies and his reverence for the music of the past were both derived from the same artistic principle—namely, that the wider one's knowledge of old music, the keener will be one's perception of the new. Fauré more than made up for the loss of Dubois by placing on the *Conseil supérieur* Debussy and d'Indy, two musicians who differed from each other as much as either of them did from their immediate predecessors[1]; and at the same time he gave his students every opportunity of learning about as wide a variety of musical history as possible, not merely a single phase of it. 'The classics' for him, in a word, did not mean only the late eighteenth and earlier nineteenth century.

After four years' directorship Fauré obtained what most previous directors had had at least as soon as their appointment—a seat in the Institut. He had made a previous bid for this in 1896, at the time of his first entry into the Conservatoire, and on that occasion was passed over in favour of Charles Lenepveu, whom M. Koechlin describes[2] as a typical trainer of Rome scholars. But now he applied for, and secured, the seat left vacant in the Académie des Beaux-Arts (one of the four academies, *other* than the Académie française itself, which together form the Institut de France) by the death of Reyer the opera composer, and formerly occupied by Berlioz. Elections of this kind are notoriously the subject of intrigues recalling the

[1] The old insult to Ravel was also avenged by employing him as an examiner.

[2] *Op. cit.*, p. 23

cardinals' college at the choice of a pope in the sixteenth century, and it is not surprising, in view of the controversies long associated with Fauré's name, that the ballot had to be taken five times before he finally emerged the victor. He himself was in Barcelona at the time, conducting his Requiem and playing his first Quintet; but the necessary canvassing was done for him partly by his father-in-law, Fremiet, and partly by the ever-helpful Saint-Saëns, who came home all the way from Algeria to press Fauré's claims among his wide and variously influential acquaintance. At last it was possible to say that something like recognition had come to Fauré, now aged sixty-four; and even something approaching financial ease, for his Conservatoire salary was supplemented to a total of 25,000 francs per year by his work on the *Figaro* and a new publishing agreement with the firm of Heugel (proprietors of the musical magazine *Le Ménestrel*) who issued his works between 1906 and 1913, after which he transferred his favour to the house of Durand. And finally, his name had become so much one to conjure with that it was adopted for the presidency of a new concert society.

The old Société Nationale had undergone certain vicissitudes since its original foundation. As early as 1886 d'Indy's suggestion that it should include foreign classics in its programmes was regarded by Saint-Saëns and Bussine as a betrayal of its main purpose, and they resigned. The wedge, against which they had protested, was not indeed driven in much farther than its thin end, for the programmes remained principally French; but as César Franck was virtually (though not nominally) president from 1886 until his death in 1890, when his place was taken by d'Indy, it is understandable that the society's policy should have come more and more to favour the works of the school attaching itself to those two masters, and in 1909 another group was organized, the Société musicale indépendante (S.M.I.) —a title adopted, apparently, from very much the same motive which induces certain hostelries in England to describe themselves as 'Free Houses'. Fauré accepted the presidency of this new society all the more willingly as he himself was not altogether in sympathy with Schola Cantorum ideals. The beneficent effect of Bordes's historical enthusiasms (paralleled, as we have seen, by Fauré's own reforms in the Conservatoire syllabus) was somewhat complicated by d'Indy's excessive regard for the Beethoven succession; Saint-Saëns thought it a little unhappy that d'Indy should, on his own showing, have taken many of his ideas on composition from Riemann, and M. Vuillermoz roundly accused him and the other Franck pupils of 'ingenuously Teutonizing our art, notwithstanding their demonstrative nationalism'.[1] Which was no doubt an over-statement; and certainly one has had occasions enough to deplore the Parisian habit, at least as old as the days of Gluck, of splitting the artistic effort of a time into two camps where no very definite rivalry really exists. Nevertheless the danger that French music should fall, belatedly, into the pit which it had hitherto been almost continentally unique in avoiding[2] must have presented itself with some force to Fauré—who was perhaps more French than some of the others in proportion as he was less chauvinistic —as well as to his younger colleagues in the S.M.I.; and we may be sure that Pierre Lalo's condemnation of the new society was a good deal more biassed in the other direction. He, quite frankly, regarded it[3] as having been founded out of pique by a few young musicians who could not have their quite inconsiderable works performed by the 'Nationale'; and he was sorry, he said, to see them thus making use of Fauré's reputation to put him up as a rival to d'Indy. However, both Fauré and d'Indy were very far from regarding the matter in that light themselves, for they remained on excellent terms of friendship until Fauré's death; and he, remembering how the Société Nationale had helped him in his younger days, reserved for it the first performances of his late chamber works. During the 1914 war the two societies combined their resources for the sake of economy. Fauré would have liked the fusion to be made permanent, but the tendencies they represented were too divergent for that,

[1] In the *Revue musicale*, special number (October 1922), quoted and translated by E. Burlingame Hill, *Modern French Music*, p. 105.
[2] See next chapter.
[3] *Le Temps*, 31st August 1910.

*B

even though Ravel, for example, was a member of both committees[1]. The truth will perhaps be found in the view, shared by M. Koechlin[2] and Mr. Burlingame Hill[3], that the competition of the younger society induced the older to adopt a broader outlook.

Fauré's triumph had its darker side. Scarcely had he arrived at a measure of official recognition than he found himself obliged to contend more and more with the progressive invasions of a major disability: he was becoming deaf. He had observed the first signs of this as early as 1903, and by 1910 it was really serious. He said as little about it as possible, partly from pure unwillingness to advertise his sorrows and partly because he could not afford to lose his professional work by announcing himself as unfit for it. Unfit in any conclusive sense, of course, he was not: the last twenty years of his life were the period of perhaps his finest achievements as a composer—four volumes of songs, a score of piano pieces revealing almost unsuspected features of his style, and six superb chamber works; but he was seldom present at the performance of any of them, for, though his deafness was never absolutely complete, it was complicated in his late years by distortion of pitch. The higher frequencies sounded to him flat, and the lower ones sharp[4], which was perhaps a symptom of the arterio-sclerosis from which he ultimately died. And it may have been hereditary, for one of his brothers had been deaf for some years.

Neither did he ever hear the largest among his works of this last period—*Pénélope*[5], his only full-length composition for the opera-house. The dramatic soprano Lucienne Bréval had in 1907 offered him the scheme for this work, the poem of which, by René Fauchois, presents the story of Ulysses's homecoming

[1] Séré, *Musiciens français d'aujourd'hui*, p. 348.

[2] *Op. cit.*, p. 35.

[3] *Op. cit.*, p. 10.

[4] Dame Ethel Smyth suffered in the same way towards the end of her life.

[5] Published, curiously, without an opus number. There are, however, in the list of his works half a dozen opus numbers under which nothing appears, and *Pénélope* would just fit No. 100 among these.

and the discomfiture of Penelope's suitors. It occupied him for the next six years, being written mainly at Lausanne during vacation periods and first produced at Monte Carlo in 1913. The people in charge of the production were not very sympathetic—what was this drama on a Greek subject doing in a place identified with all that was most ephemeral in modern fashionable life?—and on the day after the first performance Fauré wrote home that the Monte Carlo production no longer interested him except as a rehearsal for Paris.[1] In Paris it was produced the same year at a new theatre, the Champs-Élysées, under Astruc's management, Mlle. Bréval being there joined by a new tenor, Muratore, in the part of Ulysses[2], and the conductor being Louis Hasselmans, originally a violoncellist (Fauré dedicated his first cello Sonata to him). Here it fared better—at first—but the theatre did not: by the end of the year the management was bankrupt and the theatre closed; and though *Pénélope* was taken up with some success by the Monnaie at Brussels, and later at the Paris Opéra-Comique (with Claire Croiza), it has never been popular.

The last few years of Fauré's life were passed in a kind of semi-retirement, though with no slackening of his productivity as a composer. In the war period, while the German army was so dangerously near to Paris, he transferred his abode to the house of a brother who lived at Pau in the western Pyrenees. In any case his bronchial condition had become such as to require regular wintering in the south. The final and painful break with professional life came in 1920, when the Ministry of Public Instruction required him gently but inexorably to resign the Conservatoire directorship on account of his deafness. He probably reflected with some bitterness that Ambroise Thomas had held *his* post until his death, at the age of eighty-five, and with no more satisfaction that he himself, having been only twenty-four years in the service of the ministry, was not legally entitled to a pension. The government did in fact, under

[1] P. Fauré-Fremiet, *op. cit.*, p. 78.

[2] The part was played at Monte Carlo by Rousselière, who had also sung in *Prométhée*.

pressure, make him a small allowance, and furthermore softened the blow to the best of its ability by awarding him a high order in the Legion of Honour, where he had already held the rank of *commandeur* since 1910. His income was seriously diminished, and the cost of living had meanwhile risen, especially with devaluation; but evidently he had enough left to enable him, while retaining his home in Paris, to winter in small hotels on the Riviera. For the summer—the most difficult time of the year to find a beneficent climate—he enjoyed the hospitality of two devoted friends, M. and Mme. Fernand Maillot, who had a house at Annecy in Savoy, overlooking a charming lake scene.[1] Here were written, or planned, many of the works which attested to the last the creative vigour still inhabiting a body that was becoming every day more frail. Fauré's last appearance at a public concert was at Tours in 1921, where of course he had to play without listening and to keep in time with his partners by watching them; and the same year he made a last journey to his native department, visiting Montgauzy and Pamiers, where two of his cousins were still living.

A public appearance of a different kind was organized for him on 20th June 1922 by Maillot and a few other friends. They arranged a benefit concert of his works and persuaded the government to make it a national homage. It took place at the Sorbonne, and the President of the Republic, Alexandre Millerand, was there in person. The Société des Concerts du Conservatoire provided the orchestra and the choir, who performed the *Cantique de Racine* and some selections from the theatre music—*Shylock*, *Pelléas* and *Caligula*; the same orchestra was joined by Casals in the *Élégie* and by Cortot in the *Ballade*; and the conductor's desk was occupied successively by Rabaud, d'Indy, Philippe Gaubert, Büsser and Messager. Three solo singers appeared, each with a different accompanist—Claire Croiza with Cortot, Jeanne Raunay with Robert Lortat and Charles Panzéra with his wife Madeleine Baillot—contributing to the programme

[1] So that only a few months before his death he was able from Annecy to pay a visit of homage to Nyon, the native town of his old teacher Niedermeyer.

Les Berceaux, *Soir*, *Mandoline*, *Lydia*, *Aurore*, *Le Parfum impérissable* and Fauré's last vocal work, the song-cycle *L'Horizon chimérique*, which he completed that very year and dedicated to Panzéra. Lortat also played the sixth Nocturne, the fifth Barcarolle and the second Impromptu; and he joined with four string players (Tourret, Gentil, Vieux and Hekking) in the culminating feature of the concert, the second pianoforte Quintet, written only the year before but already the subject of a great ovation to Fauré at a performance in the Conservatoire. The concert lasted until one o'clock in the morning and left no doubt of the honour in which he was held by musicians and other friends young and old. Many of them combined the same year to produce a special number of the *Revue musicale*, devoted entirely to Fauré and his music.

He had two more years to live, and three more works to write. The thirteenth Nocturne, one of the most pathetically eloquent of his pieces, was his farewell to pianoforte solo writing; the Trio had the good fortune to be introduced to the public by Cortot, Thibaud and Casals; and in 1923 Fauré ventured for the first time upon a string Quartet, a form which he declared with characteristic modesty to have left alone until then on account of its great difficulty. He continued his usual round of seasonal migrations, but was becoming steadily weaker and could do only a little work each day. In the summer of 1924 he had gone to Annecy once more, and there he wrote the finale of the Quartet, turning over in his mind the possibility of inserting another movement between the first *allegro* and the *andante*, but finding himself satisfied that the work would be complete without it. His strength was so exhausted that he had to take oxygen, and that summer he stayed on at Annecy rather longer than before. But when he knew he was dying he left for Paris, resolved to live out his last hours with his family. For another fortnight he survived in his home at Passy, retouching the Quartet here and there and finally confiding the manuscript to Roger-Ducasse with the recommendation to examine it carefully and publish it 'if it were found worth playing!' It was proposed to bring the Krettly Quartet to play it in his presence, but he refused, with the sad knowledge that his affliction would have ruined the hearing of it.[1] He died at 1.50 a.m. on 4th November 1924, and his wife died less than a year after.

The government accorded him a state funeral, attended by the President of the Republic and conducted by the Archbishop of Paris from the Madeleine. The music was, fittingly, his own: first an extended improvisation by the organist on his *Élégie*, then the peaceful little Nocturne from the *Shylock* music, and for the liturgical purpose his great Requiem, after which the coffin was carried out to the strains of the *adagio* which he had written to introduce the death scene of Mélisande. Jeanne Laval and, once more, Charles Panzéra were the soloists in the Requiem. After which there were public speeches from the Minister of Public Instruction and others; and doubtless there were on that occasion some in the assembled company who learned for the first time the greatness of the musician who had departed.

Physically Fauré had many features of the southern race from which he had sprung. He was short of stature and—until his last years—extremely active of body; not that he wasted his time on physical exercises for their own sake. He had the abundant hair of a southerner, though it turned white at an early age, thus accentuating the very dark complexion which caused some of his biographers to indulge in imaginative speculations about a possible admixture of Arab blood. His portraits all show him with a drooping moustache and a little tuft of beard under the lower lip. His nose and forehead made, to judge by his portraits[2], a continuous retreating line remotely suggestive of the traditional Hellenic profile. But his general appearance seems to have conformed, without either provincial or occupational eccentricities, to the best standard of that Parisian intellectual society of which he was one of the finest examples.

[1] A similar proposal with regard to one of his Quintets from Queen Elisabeth of the Belgians (who played the violin herself and to whom Fauré dedicated his second violin Sonata) was cut short by his death. (Bruneau, *op. cit.*, p. 33.)

[2] Of which, in addition to photographs, there are three by J. S. Sargent and one by Jacques-Émile Blanche.

CHAPTER III

MUSIC IN FRANCE BEFORE FAURÉ

By the middle of the nineteenth century it had become customary throughout Europe, and particularly in countries where the evidence of any other example was either dying out altogether or confining itself to the purely rustic strata of society, to regard the art of music as something whose headquarters were in Germany, with an important but highly specialized department (the opera) in Italy. England at one end of the continent, and Russia at the other, filled their academies with German professors who taught German methods and their opera-houses with Italian singers who sang Italian works. And certainly, from the beginning of the eighteenth century onwards, musical development had come to be directed more and more by an Italo-German tradition—a kind of musical Axis, except that it centred upon Venice, or Naples, and Vienna, rather than Rome and Berlin—which eventually imposed itself with such force as to kill, and not merely to eclipse, most of its rivals. Italians might be ignorant of any music but that of their own country, Germans would more likely regard it as automatically inferior, but the result was the same: music from anywhere else tended to appear even in the sight of its own producers as outside the normal centre. The Axis has been broken—the Italian influence has waned; but in many places the German hegemony is with us yet.

This account, however, does not apply entirely to the situation in France; French music had never been completely drawn into the Italo-German orbit. The long and glorious line of *clavecinistes*, from Couperin onwards, worked out in their harpsichord pieces—nominally descriptive but really, in the most exact sense of the word, imaginative—a vein quite different from that of the partitas, fugues and toccatas of keyboard composers elsewhere; while the achievement of the French opera writers from Lully to Rameau and beyond, who constitute a line equally long and glorious, was so little akin to anything done in the Italian or German theatre that it is only now beginning to be understood in its true light. For it was the example of Rameau, more than any other external influence, which guided Gluck in his famous (and frequently misinterpreted) operatic reforms; I may here appropriately quote from one of Fauré's own *Figaro* articles in which he remarked that the French have a right to claim Gluck as, in a way, their own: among other reasons 'because the masters who pointed out to him the path which he was to follow so triumphantly—Lully and Rameau—are ours also'.[1] In fact the so-called reforms of Gluck consisted very largely in an adaptation of that same French operatic tradition which French composers were at the same time being invited by their own literary colleagues to abandon in favour of an already debased Italian model; and his achievement may well be described as having—along with a closer knitting of the dramatic outline—produced French opera with an Italian musical vocabulary: which mainly meant a vocabulary of considerably less musical interest than Rameau's own.[2] Even so, to quote again from Fauré in the *Figaro*: 'as soon as Gluck became the really great Gluck, with *Orpheus* and *Alcestis*, his own countrymen no longer understood him'; but for real individuality of melodic line and harmonic construction —such, I mean, as will strike the attention apart from the prestige of vocal execution or theatrical situation—one must turn back from Gluck to his French predecessor, which is doubtless what Debussy had seen when he made his famous protest in Rameau's favour.[3]

In the earlier half of the nineteenth century, moreover, French music continued to stand a little apart from the more widely accepted evolution—which was now in a degenerative

[1] In *Opinions musicales de Gabriel Fauré*, ed. Gheusi, p. 51.

[2] For the form of this judgment I am indebted to some unpublished researches of my friend and colleague Professor C. M. Girdlestone; and for some of its details to an essay, also unpublished, by another friend, the late Miss Eve Kisch.

[3] See Louis Laloy, *La musique retrouvée*, p. 83; also E. Lockspeiser, *Debussy*, p. 103.

direction. Scarcely had the German-Italian collaboration produced its fine flower in the 'Viennese Classics' than it fell apart, leaving each nationality free to indulge its own vice, so that Italian music tended to become mere noise and sensationalism while the Germans inclined towards mere sloppiness and *Schwärmerei.* Of romantic opera as produced under these two auspices it is difficult to determine which is the more repulsive. The one was excellently characterized by Browning in his evocation of Verdi, 'at his worst opera's end', apprehensive of the painful reaction his crudities must have aroused in one who remembered better things:

> While the mad houseful's plaudits near outbang
> His orchestra of salt-box, tongs and bones,
> He looks through all the roaring and the wreaths
> Where sits Rossini patient in his stall.[1]

—while the other, though it may show a slightly better sense of the symphonic responsibilities of its medium, is no richer in musical invention and is still less worthy (even at its best in such a work as Weber's *Freischütz*) to be an entertainment for adult intelligences. Italy during this period had little instrumental music to speak of; and that produced for German consumption leaves upon the listener, for the most part, an impression of having lain for rather too long in a tepid and enervating bath. But French taste continued to express itself along lines rather different from any of these. It is no idle coincidence that Rossini—who constitutes a link, though a sadly attenuated one, with the theatrical music of the eighteenth century—should have found on the whole a greater welcome in Paris than in his own country; for the French writers who succeeded him (those of the Auber school), deplorably superficial though they usually are, wrote for an audience which looked with suspicion both on the overheated passion of Donizetti's heroes and on the puerile supernaturalism of the Wolf's Glen. And the demand for instrumental music in France, in Napoleonic days and after, was satisfied not so much by the yearning type of composition

[1] *Bishop Blougram's Apology*, 383-6.

made unmistakably in Germany, of which Spohr is the representative (and to which Schubert also contributed), but by a number of composers of various nationalities—for France had few of her own—whose outlook was cosmopolitan and who were all the more acceptable to French musical opinion in that they had not disowned the eighteenth century to the same extent as was the case with Italian and German 'native' music. Reicha was the earliest of them, and it is significant that his harmonic experiments should have been dismissed by 'official' German opinion of the romantic age—represented here by its reflexion in successive editions of Grove's Dictionary—as having had 'no effect but to banish tonality'[1]; since the respect entertained by this official opinion for 'tonality' in the very narrowest sense was equalled only by the vehemence with which it claimed to represent an emancipation from eighteenth-century rules. Then came Kalkbrenner, whose vogue indicates how France still maintained, comparatively speaking, a line of communication with those masters of the preceding age whose influence elsewhere had waned in proportion as their names were venerated. For Kalkbrenner was a pupil of Haydn; just as Hummel—another writer whose works remained current in France as late as the present century—had been taught by Mozart, and Field[2]—whose well-known influence on Chopin derived principally from his popularity in Paris—by Clementi. Even Chopin himself—that single example in musical history of a drawing-room favourite who was also a composer of serious worth—is at any rate remarkable for having owed nothing to the German *Gemüt* or the Italian *affetto* which were elsewhere acclaimed as new lights in the art.

When Romanticism did begin to affect music in France the resultant product, furthermore, was rhetorical rather than *schwärmerisch*. Berlioz exemplifies it at the best it could ever be, and he, with his avowed German sympathies, does indeed display both features; but in some ways his was an individual

[1] Grove, *s.v.* Reicha.

[2] One of the prizes carried off by Fauré at the École Niedermeyer during the 1850s was the volume of Field's concertos.

rather than a typical talent, and the really representative composer of French romanticism was another foreigner, Meyerbeer, whose operatic writing certainly has points of contact with both Weber and Donizetti, but who stopped short of the excesses of either in the direction of naïve yearning or violent passion. He thus succeeded, at any rate, in arriving at a more satisfactory alliance with the theatre; he did not disown 'stage illusion'—I mean that *consciousness* of illusion, the exact opposite of *being illusioned*, which is so essential a part of the proper reaction to a theatrical performance—and was thus eminently suitable to the French temperament in that his work is less flagrantly disproportionate than either the German or the Italian romantic opera to the adult consciousness of a cultivated public.[1]

It may be asked, why should this prolonged attention be devoted to opera in a book dealing with a composer who avoided opera until he was over sixty? The answer is that French music cannot, at any time since the seventeenth century, be profitably discussed apart from the theatre, whose proximity is usually observable even in those musicians who were not employed in its service. Fauré himself has left an account of how he and his fellow-students at the École Niedermeyer, even though the plan of their studies excluded the opera almost as markedly as that of the Conservatoire emphasized it, used to spend their leisure hours (especially during bad weather when no other recreation was possible) in the study of operatic scores by Gluck and Mozart.[2]

[1] I think I am justified in making this generalization about French taste in spite of the fact that here and there some of the French romantics welcomed the supernatural imaginings of their German compeers. Berlioz' *Nuit de sabbat* is the work of one who stood self-confessedly a little outside the main body of French consciousness; Gautier's adaptation of the Wilis in the *Giselle* ballet was made to suit a scheme of deliberate unreality; while Franck's attempt to take a similar legend seriously, in *Le Chasseur maudit*, resulted in one of the weakest of his works.

[2] And, one must add in the interests of accuracy, by Weber also, not to mention Méhul. (See Fauré's own *Souvenirs* in the *Revue musicale* for October 1922.) See also p. 25.

It is notable moreover that the French operatic tradition, pitiable though its productions in the early and mid-nineteenth century tended to be, has yet been accountable in an indirect or a negative way for some of the better fortunes of French music at a subsequent period. To regard the matter in its most paradoxical light, one may at least point out that Debussy in his *Pelléas* and Dukas in his *Ariane* produced better works by avoiding a bad model than any of the post-Wagnerians by imitating a good one. But this is to overstate the case; for even in the nineteenth century the French opera as a form is not to be exclusively blamed for the vices of its own worst examples. We may freely admit that with Adolphe Adam and Ambroise Thomas the art of musical composition in France touched its nadir; but the tradition which they so unworthily represented was not only strong enough to survive even the onslaughts of Berlioz, even the Wagner furore—for that does not prove very much: it is true that Bizet and Massenet, in whom the tradition so quickly recovered itself, show no traces whatever of Wagner, yet the biological analogy may not legitimately be pushed to the length of supposing that because a musical stock survives it is therefore artistically healthy—but it also helped to render French music more or less immune from another, more insidious influence which elsewhere had become more and more pervasive as the century progressed.

I mean that of the Beethoven succession.

It would not be accurate to say, simply, the influence of Beethoven. The unfortunate effect to which I refer has been brought about more particularly by those *traditionalistes beethovéniens*, as M. Koechlin calls them[1], who regarded their idol as the last word in music, beyond which there was nothing but heresy; who were repelled by work such as Fauré's own because its musical language (especially on the harmonic side) had abandoned the methods of Beethoven for something more nearly approaching those of Bach; and who assumed it to be axiomatic that the somewhat limited harmonies of Beethoven were all that was generally necessary to musical salvation; so

[1] Koechlin, *Gabriel Fauré*, p. 201.

that they not only over-rated but misrepresented the composer they were celebrating. And their effective force—encouraged, one has to admit, by the misplaced emphasis of certain of Beethoven's own pronouncements upon the value and significance of his work—made itself felt over a considerable part of Europe, for the greater part of the century, in both composition and criticism. It is almost platitudinous to say that the nineteenth century was musically dominated by Beethoven; and, like most truisms, it conveys rather less than half the truth. What is not always realized is that the prevailing wind in nineteenth-century musical weather was not simply Beethoven, but Beethoven at his worst. His really valuable significance is even now partly obscured by the undiscriminating adulation of him which has become a fashion since a generation after his own day; and his influence on subsequent musical development was almost uniformly deplorable, because it was exercised by means of his least admirable works. The low level to which the average of critical sense had sunk in the musical world of sixty or seventy years ago is nowhere more forcibly attested than by the pious horror aroused by anyone who recognized that the influence was deplorable or that any of Beethoven's works might not be admirable. Neither is the twentieth century in very much better case; even so deservedly influential a critic as Sir Donald Tovey was not above quoting the 'pitying smile' reserved by Joachim for 'those inexperienced composers who would not learn from any Beethoven other than the last quartets'[1]—a pity which we can very easily survive when we remember that the penalty for learning from middle-period Beethoven is to write like Joachim.

And the bulk of mid-nineteenth-century composition shows how fully the penalty was paid. For the greater part of the century the Beethoven who commanded general allegiance was neither the arresting young successor to Haydn, who in such works as the D minor Sonata (Op. 31, No. 2) or the C minor Concerto (Op. 37) bade fair to extend the vocabulary and enrich the syntax of the 'Viennese masters' to a greater degree than

[1] Tovey, *Essays in Musical Analysis*, Vol. III, *s.v.* Joachim, Hungarian Concerto.

any of their other pupils; nor the solitary pioneer of the late chamber music, whose example would have been pregnant for the development of an age not already determined to abandon purely artistic significance in favour of a direct appeal to the coarser perceptions of mankind. Instead, the admiration of average opinion in that age was lavished on those works which (as, for example, long stretches of the 'Pastoral' Symphony and the 'Waldstein' Sonata) seem unaware of the existence of any harmony beyond tonic and dominant; or which make desperate efforts to find an 'expressive' value in sheer repetitiveness[1]; or whose heavy-handed unsubtlety (as in the seventh Symphony, or the choral finale of the ninth) is all too worthy of the vulgarian expansiveness which it so frequently illustrated. This was the aspect of Beethoven most observable in his admirers, not only the critics who guided public opinion but also those composers who were most evidently his disciples, such as Schubert and the earlier Wagner; both these groups contributing extensively to the triumph of that combination of romantic sentiment with undistinguished mentality, which rendered the middle of the nineteenth century a 'record low', as the Americans would call it, in the history of musical taste.

With so long a fashion thus set for sententious commonplace and harmonic timidity, it became increasingly plain (for those who had ears to hear) that little further music of even initial merit, let alone front-rank value, could be written until a release was found from the post-Beethovenian diatonicism, and in particular from the assumptions involved in the rule of the leading-note, which becomes intolerable to a sensitive musical ear in proportion as it is accepted for an axiom by coarsened senses and commonplace perceptivities. Here even Beethoven at his best was no help; for even when he exceptionally adumbrated an addition to the musical vocabulary he did not match it with the fresh developments of syntax which it demanded. The augmented triad, for example, which he threw out tentatively

[1] This determination to 'extract the last drop from a foregone conclusion' is so frequent throughout the middle-period works that I need hardly quote examples.

towards the end of the fugue in the third Rasumovsky Quartet was still locked to a basis of dominant-to-tonic, the augmented fifth serving merely as a reinforcement of the leading-note; so that although the chord was included in the traditional harmony of the academic textbooks, it had so to speak to be discovered over again before it could be used for such 'deliverances from bondage' as this in Fauré's second violin Sonata:

It is a curious fact that the nineteenth century, which liked to advertise itself as an age of musical emancipation, remained hide-bound—not only in its academic but also in its romantic music[1]—by an exclusive leading-note diatonicism which one is all the more inclined to trace to the Fux-Albrechtsberger school of theorists because no real justification for it can be found in the eighteenth-century composers themselves; not even in the comparatively restricted vocabulary of the 'Viennese' classics, still less in that of Bach and his contemporaries.

Of course the musical language spoken in France during the same period was in general as unadventurous as elsewhere; but what made France a likely raising-ground for something better was that although her music was as much sunk in commonplace as that of any other country, her composers were at least not emphatic about it and did not proceed on the assumption that by treating the obvious in a portentous manner they would save it from being obvious. The familiarity of the French public with Boïeldieu's or Adolphe Adam's innocent tinklings, for example, did not predispose it against Chopin in the way that so many

[1] For the 'Philistines' so justly attacked by Schumann—Herz and the rest—belonged rather to the latter category.

Germans were predisposed against Wagner.[1] In France the banalities of the post-Beethovenian idiom, which even Schumann found inadequate for his purposes, had not been propounded with the force of prophecy; except perhaps by Berlioz—which explains in part why the general run of *his* work is harmonically uninteresting. It may be freely admitted that the descent from Rameau, for whom 'harmony was the very stuff of music'[2], to Boïeldieu or Hérold was little short of pitiable; but at any rate the French were not deceived into accepting a more portentously-presented music as essentially any less banal. It was indeed by an exaggeration of this very critical virtue that they were unjustly cold in their reception of Berlioz himself. The nearest they came to being taken in was in their welcome to Meyerbeer, who momentarily imposed himself on their acceptance, as much by his sense of the theatre as because his music was noisy and 'fruity' enough to suit the romantic temperament; but when this also was shown up for the bombastic thing that it is, the Meyerbeer vogue declined with it. Vociferousness cannot permanently conceal poverty of substance, at all events from those who are not normally predisposed to accept the manner of presentation of an art for its inner essence.

No doubt it was because French taste remained fundamentally inapt for persuasion by virtuosity of sentiment—for Liszt, the next foreign visitor to capture the Parisian fancy, was a virtuoso rather in the usual technical sense—that France recovered from romanticism somewhat sooner than most other nations. Certainly, by the time of Fauré's pupil age, something like the French tradition had reasserted itself, which may not have been any better than the typical German music of the time, and which was doubtless considerably inferior to the highest peaks of Schumann or the youthful promise of Brahms, but whose claim on our gratitude is that it stood less in the way of what Fauré had to give. His characteristic achievement was to be, with a renewed idiom, upon lines very similar to those of the eighteenth-

[1] It will be remembered that Wagner's bitterest opponent, Hanslick, had been the prophet of Beethoven and Schubert.

[2] I quote again from Eve Kisch: see p. 40.

century classic masters; and any education based mainly on the Beethoven succession would have acted as an obstacle to this, just as in Germany itself it prevented the revival of interest in Bach, undertaken by Schumann and Mendelssohn, from essentially affecting the evolution of German composition. The models, on the other hand, which Fauré found established in his youth, did not prevent him either from ranging in his studies over a wide field of music in past ages[1] or from becoming in his own person one of the first of the moderns. One survivor from a previous generation, who had lived on in France to a revered old age, was Rossini—whose lasting reputation among the French of that day is not without bearing on his rediscovery by certain leading musicians of our own time, heralded as early as 1914 in Sir Osbert Sitwell's description of his *Can-can* as 'that first clear gem of modern music'[2]. The place in theatrical music formerly occupied by Auber (who had become a kind of operatic Elder Statesman and did not die until 1871) was now filled by Gounod, as much an exploiter of emotions as any of his German or Italian contemporaries, but with whom the emotions exploited were taken from recognizable life rather than from the world of dreams and substitute-living[3], as may be immediately understood by comparing his Marguerite either with impossible ministering angels like Weber's Agathe and Wagner's Elisabeth or with the glamorous spiritual courtesans of the type of Verdi's Violetta. From the purely musical point of view, moreover,

[1] I may remind my readers that Fauré as director of the Conservatoire attached great importance to the study of as many phases of the older music as possible, not merely of one (see p. 31); and that the habit of regarding all pre-nineteenth-century music as so archaic that it needs modernizing, in order to render it acceptable to modern audiences, is one belonging pre-eminently to the Germany of the post-Beethovenian period.

[2] In the volume of stories entitled *Triple Fugue*, ed. of 1927, p. 158.

[3] The German objection to Gounod's *Faust* is based, one suspects, not so much on the shifting of balance in favour of Marguerite as on the elimination by Gounod of any atmosphere of unreality, so that even Mephistopheles is no longer a 'metaphysical' figure.

Gounod was an improvement on Auber, much as Delibes, in the realm of the ballet, represented a better standard than that of his teacher Adam. With regard to the former I may quote a judgment of Maurice Ravel:

> The real founder of song-writing in France was Charles Gounod. It was the musician of *Venise*, of *Philémon et Baucis* and of the shepherd's song in *Sapho* who rediscovered the secret of an harmonic sensuality which had been lost since the French harpsichordists of the seventeenth and eighteenth centuries.[1]

and upon the latter, a few lines of Octave Séré:

> Into a hitherto casually treated *genre* [*i.e.* that of the ballet] Delibes brought a dignity and vigour of style, a spaciousness of form and a richness of instrumentation unknown before. He was the first to introduce symphonic music into the ballet, while at the same time remaining quite French.[2]

In the matter of smaller-scale vocal and pianoforte works the only one of the exclusively German composers who impigned at all notably upon native French music was the best of them, Schumann, whose sense of musical invention was far ahead of any other writer of *Lieder* and *Charakterstücke* in the romantic period; otherwise the prevailing memory in instrumental music was that of the generation of 'Viennese masters' pupils' previously discussed, which had been fortified and extended in its scope by Chopin. In the concerted forms a musician's training,

[1] From the article on Fauré's songs, reported from Rave by Roland-Manuel in the *Revue musicale* for October 1922; quoted and translated by E. Burlingame Hill, *Modern French Music*, p. 45. I have, however, altered one phrase in the translation given by Mr. Hill; even an American, it seems, may not only confuse the verbs *instaurer* and *restaurer*, but also be misled by the fact that the best French usage now calls vocal works on a small scale by the name of *mélodies* and not *lieder* (see p. 57).

[2] Séré, *Musiciens français d'aujourd'hui*, p. 151.

apart from the salutary example he would find to his hand in Mendelssohn's chamber works, was doubtful, for France had still no tradition of instrumental ensemble; but here Fauré was fortunate to have been taught at the Niedermeyer by Saint-Saëns, who, though his own predilections as a virtuoso performer led him to incline too much towards Liszt, and though he seems, by the very force of his own international sympathies, to have been somewhat affected by the Beethovenolatry of his time—so that Philippe Fauré-Fremiet can even write of him as having 'introduced into France the Beethovenian conception of music, at a period when French art was dominated by the influence of Rossini, Auber and Ambroise Thomas'[1]—yet had a sufficiently wide outlook not to treat the whole history of music as though it converged upon the figure of a single master, and was, in particular, eminently responsible for propagating the cult of Bach. It will be remembered that Debussy's 'Monsieur Croche' found most worthy of remembrance, among all Saint-Saëns's achievements as a musical educator, that he 'helped to make Liszt and his tumultuous genius known, and that he worshipped the good old Bach'; and this at a time when the average of criticism in Germany itself was of an almost uniform short-sightedness, so that it was next to impossible to open a German critical edition of Mozart without seeing his work described as that of a 'precursor', while the German attitude towards Bach was seldom as circumspect as that of W. H. Riehl[2], whose question 'What would old Bach have said if he could have heard a Beethoven symphony?'[3] followed by a similar query as to what our ancestors of coaching days would have said at the sight of a railway train, indicated that the reaction might as well have been one of dismay as of admiration. Saint-Saëns on the other hand—as befitted the man who was afterwards to edit Rameau's works with a salutary absence of modernization—was evidently in full sympathy with the aims of the Niedermeyer school, the catholicity of whose

[1] P. Fauré-Fremiet, *Gabriel Fauré*, p. 35.

[2] An author who combined a Munich professorship in social history with a distinguished career as historical novelist and musicologist.

[3] Riehl, *Der Zopf des Herrn Guillemain* (1863), intro.

curriculum must have been a model for its day. Through the good offices of the school Fauré, as his son expresses it, 'acquired a complete knowledge of our religious art, and lived in communion with the French and German classics.'[1] And he always looked back with gratitude upon his education there:

> In 1853 the masterpieces of J. S. Bach, which constituted our daily bread, had still not found their way into the organ class at the Conservatoire; and in the pianoforte classes at the same Conservatoire the students still laboured at the performance of Herz's concertos, while Adolphe Adam shed his brilliant light upon his composition class![2]

Evidently the Conservatoire—an institution notorious, until Fauré himself came to direct its destinies, for being far in arrear of the best taste of its own country—had just got round to where German taste had been in the 1830s.

The reference to religious art, a few lines above, reminds us of one other supremely important influence brought to bear on Fauré during the impressionable years: that of the ecclesiastical or 'Gregorian' modes. He himself wrote in the highest terms of the benefit he had derived from his training under Niedermeyer's own system in the accompaniment of plainchant on the organ,

> according to a method, placed for the first time upon a rational basis, and nowadays adopted in most churches, but of very recent growth at that time, since it was due to the initiative of Niedermeyer himself in collaboration with the learned musicographer Joseph d'Ortigues.[3]

The work of these two has been somewhat blown upon by subsequent researches; partly, I think, from the motive of a purism which objects to giving plainchant any accompaniment at all—and to that extent unfairly, as it seems to me, for after years of familiarity I am as convinced as ever that plainchant

[1] P. Fauré-Fremiet, *op. cit.*, p. 27.

[2] Gabriel Fauré, *Souvenirs* (*Revue musicale*, *loc. cit.*).

[3] *Ibid.*

implies its own harmonic background[1]—and partly because it was doubtless as imperfect as the similar pioneer work of Helmore in England. But it also resembles Helmore in that for the first time, after a period of progressive deformation extending from the late sixteenth century to the early nineteenth, plainchant was delivered from the strait-jacket of leading-note diatonicism in which successive generations of musicians in the age of the major scale had more and more closely confined it. Thus its importance for the modern musical world was revealed; for not only did this deliverance from anachronistic notions of cadence help to discover the true structure of plainchant, but (*vice versa*) the discovery of plainchant helped to convince sensitive musicians of the gratuitous impoverishment of their art for which the tonic-and-dominant obsession and its ubiquitous leading-note had been responsible. The origin of this obsession was, apparently, a feeling—which one is tempted to trace to sheer aural laziness—that modulation, *i.e.* movement towards a different note of the scale as the pivotal point of a melody, sounded unconvincing unless it were reinforced by a semitone accidental which should emphasize the position of the new tonic by an obvious pointing at it; otherwise the same kind of laziness would counsel the singer not to shift the tonic at all. This led first of all to those modifications of pure modalism known as *musica ficta*, then to the evolution of the major-scale system, concurrently with which came a minor scale so corrupted from its earliest appearance that its seventh degree was assimilated to that of the major by means of a sharpened semitone which even in its official designation was never more than an accidental. What there was to do with this restricted language was done with wonderful grace and resourcefulness in the age of Mozart. But though the motive of the diatonic evolution may have been the search for variety, its ultimate effect was one of the flattest monotony, as was observed with varying degrees of conscious-

[1] So that I cannot agree with Dr. R. O. Morris that 'there is no such thing as modal harmony', because I do not believe either in the existence of melody which implies no harmony or in the inevitability of cadential progressions.

ness by numerous composers from the mid-nineteenth century onwards, especially French[1], and stated in so many words by Gerard Manley Hopkins in a protest against the ideas of 'official' musicians in his time:

> What they call the key of the dominant, viz. one in which the fourth of the tonic is sharpened, I say is not the key of the dominant (which is in another mode than the key of the tonic and has no leading note) but the key of the tonic misplaced and transposed. . . . What he calls variety I call sameness, because modulation reduces all the rich diatonic keyboard with its six or seven authentic, not to speak of plagal, modes, to one dead level of major.[2]

The wheel had come full circle; the revival of the modes served to release music from the rigid bounds within which it had been cramped by 'tempered tonality', or leading-note diatonicism. And it is worth noting that M. Koechlin attributed to Fauré's training in 'Gregorian' music his skill in that very matter of modulation for whose sake it had originally been abandoned:

> His tonalities, clear as they are, sometimes are established very quickly and for a passing moment only—a practice observable in the sixteenth century and favoured by familiarity with the ancient modes, because they allow greater flexibility in modulation.[3]

One may see how right Hopkins was in his contention (for this is what it amounts to) that what we have called 'modulation' in the 'tempered' sense is better described not as modulation at all but as transposition—transposition of the same tonal-and-semitonal succession to a different level of pitch; and how great

[1] And, one might add, Russian; but in *their* musical background the modal tradition had not been so completely lost as to require deliberate revival.

[2] Quoted by W. H. Mellers in *Scrutiny*, Vol. xii, No. 2, p. 126 (spring 1944).

[3] Koechlin, *op. cit.*, pp. 162-3.

an enrichment of the art would derive from the newly-acquired freedom to range over a real variety of scales in which modulation should really involve a different order of degrees.

How ready (by comparison) French composers were to profit by this freedom may be observed, in an elementary way, even in such things as the recitative section of a work written frankly for popular consumption, Godard's celebrated *Berceuse de Jocelyn*; and though in France, as elsewhere, it remained customary to teach harmony as though 'tempered tonality' were the invariable norm—so that even so late an arrival at the Conservatoire as Maurice Emmanuel got into trouble with the authorities for his modal leanings[1]—yet, as M. Koechlin very rightly observes[2], a certain sympathy towards 'Gregorian' music may be observed not only in Franck and his pupils, the founders of the Schola Cantorum, but even in Lalo and Saint-Saëns, and most of all in the great teacher Bourgault-Ducoudray, whose enthusiasm for the ecclesiastical modes was increased by the affinity he had detected in them with the modes of ancient Greek music. Nowadays when every successive study brings fresh proofs of this affinity[3], we may be permitted a certain latitude in the conclusions we draw from it, so far at least as to suggest that the modes, as they undoubtedly helped Fauré to his position as a great dispeller of the German legend in music—for the undue perpetuation of leading-note diatonicism was mainly the work of the musical Axis to which I referred at the beginning of this chapter—counted also for something in his progress from a pupil in the Gregorian school to the composer of Hellenic serenity and luminosity that he was afterwards to become.

[1] Koechlin, *op. cit.*, p. 162, n.

[2] *Id.*, p. 162.

[3] See, in particular, the chapter by Professor J. F. Mountford in Powell's *New Chapters in Greek Literature* second series; also Miss Kathleen Schlesinger's contributions on the subject to *The Music Review*, 1944.

CHAPTER IV

THE SONGS

FAURÉ's position in the history of song-writing owes something of its importance to the fact that he put on the musical map what was in essence a new form. His contemporaries were well enough acquainted with what the French call *romances*, and for half a century before his time the public attention had been drawn with increasing insistence to the *Lieder* of the German composers; but here, for the first time in the history of the voice-and-keyboard lyric, was something that could not properly be included under either classification. Some of Fauré's earliest songs, certainly, are little more than *romances*, and in the 1880s it was frequent enough to see others, which obviously were not *romances*, described as *lieder* for want of a better current term[1]; but we shall see that their value depends in reality on qualities which are not those of the *Lieder* at all.

The word *romance* corresponds to the English 'ballad', and has modified its meaning across the ages in much the same way as its English counterpart; that is to say, a word originally applicable to a piece of minstrelsy, celebrating some heroic or at least forceful deed, has now come to describe a song produced for the discreet delectation of a society for which primitive violence is a foreign experience. A modern *romance*, like a modern ballad, is so adapted to the needs of drawing-room culture that it seldom escapes simpering; this is true even of such relatively superior examples of the type as the *Bergerettes* collected and adapted by Weckerlin. The general appeal of Mendelssohn's famous pianoforte pieces to such a drawing-room audience as I am describing is excellently characterized by the fact that the French name for them is *Romances sans paroles*. The vocal *romance* corresponds in fact to the album-lyric of which the romantic age

[1] Even Pierre Lalo, the music critic of *Le Temps*, who wrote with such intelligent enthusiasm for Fauré's work, consistently referred to his songs as *lieder*—and this a good deal later than the 1880s.

FAURÉ AT THE MADELEINE ORGAN

of poetry provided such a profusion of examples; and it is more or less essential that it should be constructed according to a ystem of basically identical 'verses'.

This in the eighteenth century was also true of the *Lied* in Germany—one of Goethe's earliest publications was a book of lyrics provided with tunes on such a model by B. T. Breitkopf; nd the type appears also in such things as Mozart's *An die Einsamkeit.* A growing consciousness that the metrical similarity of verses did not necessarily mean a similarity of mood in the vords of each, towards the turn of the eighteenth to the nineteenth century, brought about the development of the *durchkomponiertes Lied*, in which the musical outline follows the nood rather than the metre, thus doing away with the system of verses', or, as the French call them, *couplets.* Both forms of ong are found in Schubert, whereas the German song-writers rom Schumann onwards have devoted their attention almost xclusively to the *durchkomponiertes Lied*; but the development f this form has had little appreciable influence on the French *mélodie*—to use the name that was finally agreed upon for the ind of song of which Fauré and his contemporary Duparc vere the first great masters.

For the *Lieder*, however they may differ structurally from heir predecessors, are in essence no less naïve. The type was eveloped in Germany at a time when romantic artists and heorists of art were urging that poetry and music should be nade to appeal at the least sophisticated level of intelligence; vhen the publication of a collection of ancient popular poetry, alled *Des Knaben Wunderhorn*, was encouraging modern poets o write along the same lines; when German art readily assumed n *in modo leggendario* form as of a grandmother's tales by the reside; so that 'a whole metaphysic of naturalism'[1] enveloped he *Lied* with its ideas upon 'the instinctive expression of emotions', and a premium was put on the ingenuous and the naïve in uch a way that it very easily became merely sentimental.

'Sentimental' is a word loosely used, and it would be easy to nd examples of its use by different authors to describe almost

[1] Jankélévitch, *Gabriel Fauré et ses mélodies*, p. 2.

C

diametrically opposed types of art. But the essence of sentimentality seems to me to lie in the derivation of a specific pleasure from the contemplation of feelings—one's own or another's—regarded as a primary material of artistic satisfaction, independently of the object or the occasion that has produced them. A sentimental poem is therefore one which announces as its sole object the description of a state of feeling, considered as worthy of notice in and for itself; and similarly sentimental music is that which concentrates upon the 'rendering' of a state of emotional excitement, so that it will invite the collaboration of emotional inflexions and illustrative action in performance. The majority of *Lieder* rather imply such an invitation, and most of our celebrated *Lieder* singers are only too well aware of the fact; but a Fauré *mélodie* would be ruined by treatment on such lines.

A poem will most surely be saved from sentimentality by using no words which directly describe a feeling—it is noteworthy that the most penetrating poetry is that which confines itself to characterizing an occasion, not the feeling aroused by the occasion, and also that such a poetic procedure (that of Housman's 'Bredon Hill', for example) is found only in highly civilized ages, not at periods when 'nature', 'simplicity' and 'popular inspiration' are the watchwords—for the instinct of naïve humanity is, precisely, not to state such direct perceptions of objects but to express feelings about them.

In the same way, music will most surely escape sentimentality by not using sounds which attempt to recall in their inflexions the accents of emotionally affected speech or movement. I remember an article in *The Musical Times* of June 1934 by Mr. A. J. B. Hutchings, who put his finger on just this danger by comparing a phrase of Delius to the 'Ah!' that so frequently occurs in would-be 'expressive' poetry. I think he was unjust in that his example was badly chosen—I cannot find that Delius was often guilty of the fault in question—but he could have rendered the truth of his observation all the more telling by substituting examples drawn almost at random from the writers of *Lieder*; as indeed he did by implication, later in his article.

The history of Fauré's songs is that of a progress which for the most part was not beset by this particular danger. His genius is shown rather by the distance he travelled from the *romance de salon*; for this, and not the popular models which produced the *Lied*, was his point of departure. 'The rebirth of French music came in a country whose old-established civilization rendered it unnecessary that she should consult her archives in order to form an idea of her own destiny.'[1] In other words, the organized culture of France never having quite lost touch with the higher artistic achievements of the French, it was not necessary to assist the rebirth of French music by treating it as a 'revival', least of all a revival of 'popular' inspiration. And so it came about that the music of Fauré, and of his contemporaries and successors, was free to explore the farthest subtleties of artistic invention—a fact which has laid it open to being attacked for 'preciosity' by those who cannot apprehend what is not dinned into their ears in words of one syllable or their musical equivalent.

It is significant that the only *Lieder*-composer whose work has had much influence in France should have been Schumann[2] —for he was the only one among the pioneers of German song-writing who to any considerable extent (and *he* not always) concentrated upon musical as distinct from sentimental features; on features, that is, which form all the better a musical parallel to the text because they have an existence independent of its immediate requirements, and which 'illustrate' the words all the better for not being an 'extension' of them. A vocal line, whose chief virtue is that it follows the inflexions of the words and enables the singer to produce his sounds with accents corresponding to the feelings which the words describe—and that is the kind of vocal line demanded by the text of most *Lieder*, even a great many of Schumann's own and still more of Schubert's—may nevertheless either fail to provide a musical equivalent for the essential matter of the poem, or on the other

[1] Jankélévitch, *op. cit.*, p. 3.

[2] 'The name of Schubert', wrote Jean Chantavoine in the *Ménestrel* for 14th November 1924, 'has also been mentioned in connexion with Fauré: which indicates a complete misunderstanding of both composers'.

hand may succeed so well in conveying a *sentimental* meaning that its quality as music will be as poor as the quality of the text as poetry. But Schumann's superiority over his fellows consists mainly in his having recognized, by his keen sense of musical texture, that a phrase of music may provide an apt translation of the mood of a poem (as distinct from a sentimental imitation of its resultant emotions) without exactly fitting the outline of the words; which explains not only his sympathetic treatment of the pianoforte part—a feature of his writing very early recognized in appreciations of him—but also his harmonic enterprise, as for example in *Frauenliebe und Leben*, and his success with secondary melodies, which the voice echoes and transforms according to the limitations of the text; a feature which is noticeable moreover in the solo vocal writing of Bach, and which Fauré carried to such triumphal lengths in such songs as *Clair de lune* and *Arpège*.

This, however, is to anticipate; and the Schumann influence is not noticeable in Fauré's songs until his style was already sufficiently well formed to be able to assimilate only the best that Schumann had to offer it. The model most easily discernible in his earliest songs is that of Gounod, some of whose operatic music (*e.g.* the duet in Act III of *Faust*) he never ceased to admire, and whose songs are the apotheosis of the *romance*, though one or two of them, such as *Venise*, are so much in advance of his own usual standards as to sound not unlike the early work of Fauré himself.[1] Fauré's own Op. 1, No. 1, *Le Papillon et la fleur*, set to a simpering text by Victor Hugo, dates no doubt from his student days—perhaps indeed from the age of fifteen—and, after an introduction whose archness must be heard to be believed, settles down to a succession of *couplets* whose chief virtue is a negative one: he does not, at any rate, falsify the verbal rhythm by unauthorized repetition, as even Fauré's master Niedermeyer had thought himself at liberty to do in his celebrated setting of *Le Lac*, in which Lamartine's last line appears thus:

'Tout dise: ils ont aimé! tout dise, tout dise: ils ont aimé!'

[1] Koechlin, *Gabriel Fauré*, p. 49 and n.

thus fulfilling the singer's demand for a rhetorical ending. *Le Papillon et la fleur* had a certain success with performers, as is shown by the number of arrangements and transcriptions of it in the Hamelle catalogue, and one can understand that Fauré himself retained a certain affection for this first-fruit of his Muse; but at this distance it merits no other comment than the sketch drawn by Saint-Saëns on the original manuscript, in which the butterfly pulls a long nose at the flower. Among the other songs which form the first eight opus numbers, written at various and now no longer exactly verifiable dates in the 1860s, there are several which at any rate announce the characteristic procedures that were to come—the *Sérénade toscane* with its tritonic cadence, *Au bord de l'eau* with its consecutive sevenths, the suspended and anticipated harmonies of the *Chant d'automne*, and the easy recovery of the tonic from long distances in *Aubade*; and if the *Chanson du pêcheur*, on the celebrated poem by Gautier, seems less characteristic (its melody is unusually declamatory for Fauré), still it marks a further emancipation from the Gounodian *romance* and contributed to prepare the way for such things as the *Élégie* for violoncello, with which it has points in common —especially in its instrumental transcription under the title of *Lamento.* (A *Lamento* differs from a lament, somewhat as an elegiac from an elegy; the Italian word has in this connexion something of the extended significance attaching to the conventional Italian marks of tempo or dynamics, in accordance with which an *Allegro* is something much more generalized than a piece in *merry mood.*)

The outstanding items in this early group of songs are *Lydia* and *Après un rêve.* The latter has become almost popular in this country, though still not in accordance with its deserts as compared with certain other favourites of the concert platform; the sub-dominant-ninth chord which is the pivotal point of its first phrase:

and the ease with which syllables find their place in rhythmic groups, balancing the *melismata* upon a single syllable with which so many of its phrases end, all help to make this song a model of true eloquence such as even Fauré himself seldom surpassed. The words of *Après un rêve* were adapted by Romain Bussine from a poem in the Tuscan dialect; those of *Lydia* are by Leconte de Lisle after Horace, and the difference between the two songs is rather the difference as it appears to us (not necessarily in exact accordance with what it is as a matter of historical fact) between the modern Italian and the ancient Roman world; the one is languorous, the other serene. *Lydia* is also noteworthy for the first appearance in Fauré's work of a melodic phrase rising through the intervals of the tritone:

which was to recur in other compositions. There can be no doubt, by the way, that Fauré intended a delicate pun on the name of Lydia by choosing the key of F and beginning the melody in the Lydian mode.

To the same period belongs the *Cantique de Racine*, a setting (originally for mixed chorus, harmonium and strings, but found also as a solo) of one of the devotional poems written by the great tragic poet towards the end of his life; its kinship with the 'sacred songs' of Gounod and the anthems of Mendelssohn is obvious, but it is redeemed—as, after all, its models are to a certain degree—by a sureness of linear construction which saves it from flabbiness if not from a certain pallor.

When we reach the songs which Hamelle published as Fauré's second collected volume (afterwards reducing them from twenty-five to twenty in order to use six of them[1] in a third volume of twenty) we find the composer advancing rapidly towards a much greater sureness both of himself and of the texts which would best serve to call forth his qualities as a composer. The three songs Op. 18, with which the collection leads off, are officially dated 1880; and though a certain amount of post-dating has probably taken place with these and other works—written at a time when publishers, understandably enough, would not be particularly eager to snap up the compositions of this comparatively unknown organist as soon as they appeared—yet they carry unmistakable signs that we are already approaching the mature Fauré, whose maturity indeed had almost announced itself in advance by the two great chamber works, the violin Sonata Op. 13 and the pianoforte Quartet Op. 15. And his increasing sureness of taste in the choice of words to set is shown by the appearance, in the list of poets upon whom he drew, not only of Armand Silvestre but of Leconte de Lisle and of Verlaine, with whose collaboration some of his greatest triumphs were later to be scored. Leconte de Lisle provided the text for only five altogether of his hundred songs, but every one of the five is a masterpiece; and though the influence of Silvestre may be described as still part of his apprenticeship, yet it was an influence which at least set him on his own truest path, rather than deflecting him from it, as that of Victor Hugo had rather tended to do.

The vogue of this prestigious but unequal poet was such that many composers seem to have been impelled by the mere weight of his reputation to set his words to music; but he was not the author for Fauré. Liszt had probably suited him better than most—his expansive and slightly inflated style exactly matched the composer of the song *O quand je dors* and the symphonic poem *Ce qu'on entend sur la montagne*—but the parallel with Liszt is perhaps an exact indication of Hugo's own deficiencies. He was no encouragement to a composer whose best qualities

[1] This, of course, left only nineteen of the original collection; the gap was filled by the inclusion of an earlier song, *Barcarolle* (Op. 7, No. 3), which for some reason had not appeared in the first volume.

lay in the direction of containing and resolving his emotions rather than allowing them to overflow. Of the setting for chorus and orchestra (Op. 12) of Hugo's *Les Djinns* M. Koechlin can only say that its grandiloquence and its quite uncharacteristic harmony leave us with a feeling of surprise that it should be by Fauré at all.[1] And in general the department of Hugo's work which offers itself to musicians is the least calculated to repay their attentions. The lozenge shape of *Les Djinns* (lines of two syllables increasing to lines of ten and back again) can hardly be reproduced in music; neither was Fauré the man to subscribe uncritically to the admiration for Hugo's Gothic imaginings which had still not subsided when he began to write. Even Franck in a similar mood could write a *Chasseur maudit*, even Duparc a *Lénore*; but, apart from this youthful essay, it was Fauré who marked the deliverance of French music from the orgy of witches' sabbaths which romanticism had bequeathed to it.[2] Not for him, then, the vociferous sonorities of a Hugo; maybe indeed the *sonorous* quality in Hugo's verse is so important that it is inclined to quarrel with *musical* sonority—which would explain its unsuitability to such music as Fauré's, one of whose outstanding qualities is that it produces most of its effect by an exploitation of the varieties of sonority and not of the *inflexions* so dear to a sentimentally inclined musician. The verse of Leconte de Lisle, on the other hand, demands that 'expression' shall be *resolved* into form; and never was this done more exquisitely than in *Nell* (Op. 18, No. 1), a glorification at once of summer weather and of love's delight, whose irresistible movement is due largely to a series of modulations which avoid the conventional close while at the same time not producing the jerk of surprise that one finds in an interrupted cadence properly so called.

For nine out of the dozen songs following this one Fauré took his text from Armand Silvestre, a writer who somehow managed to combine a gift for sensitive if rather facile verse with an inexhaustible flow of 'spicy' short stories, but who proved more profitable to the composer than this description might imply. Doubtless the Silvestre settings are not among

[1] *Op. cit.*, 69-70.

[2] See Jankélévitch, *op. cit.*, 6.

Fauré's most lasting work; the 12-8 rhythm of *Le Pays des rêves* is not altogether free from a suggestion of the 'swing songs' which towards the end of last century shared a fashion with hammocks and croquet, *Notre amour* is still under the influence of the ballad-form which required among other things a top-note just before the end, while the comparison of a perished flower to a dead love in *Fleur jetée* might have been more discreetly served than by an accompaniment recalling alternately Schubert's *Erlkönig* and Saint-Saëns's 'Mon cœur s'ouvre à ta voix'. But the best of them, *Le Secret* and *Aurore*, require none of these qualifying comments. *Le Secret* is Fauré's earliest success with the key of D flat, and at the same time the tonality seems to be wavering from a signature of five flats to one of four, on account of the important function of the triad of the third degree in the pianoforte part and the G natural confirming it in the vocal line:

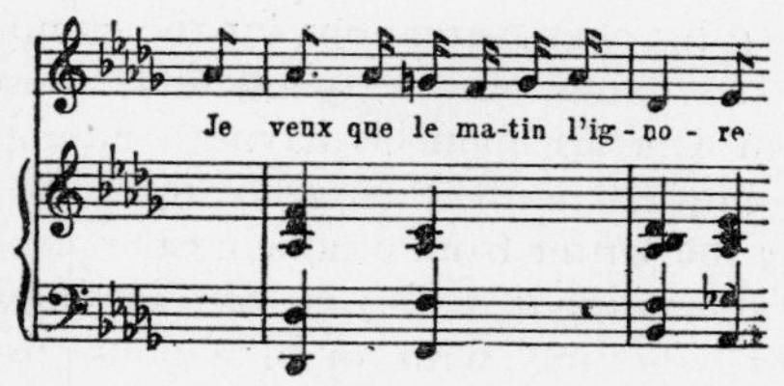

Aurore repeats under slightly different conditions the success of *Nell*—the poem, treating in this case of the dawn after a night of love, requires a less impulsive movement, even when the crotchet rhythm of the first page gives way to semiquavers; and in this song the flat seventh, so fruitful a source of originality in Fauré, makes a triumphant appearance in both melodic line and harmonic scheme, thus investing the musical movement with an interest which had long since ceased to attach to anything involving the leading-note. Both of these songs are in their way *romances de salon* sublimated to the highest degree; *Aurore* even contains the phrase 'le jardin de mon cœur' (not indeed that the 'party piece' associations of these words are such in French as to kill them in the way their English equivalent has been killed); but it is important to notice how the sublimation was effected—by eliminating the *naïveté* of the model, which moreover was a *naïveté* of a different kind from that of the *Lieder*. For theirs consisted in an acceptance of sentimental *illusions*, so that the typical 'Wanderer' or 'ingenuous lover' of German lyricism can really believe that his halting confidences are a guide to the eternal verities; whereas the *romance de salon* accepted rather a certain compound of sentimental *conventions*, and is not thus debarred by its own constitution from seeing through its own limitations. A convention is sooner thrown off than an illusion; and so it came about that Fauré was free to explore the subtlest reserves of civilized sensibility at a time when even such a late-comer to the German tradition as Brahms gives the impression that *Des Knaben Wunderhorn* is still rather embarrassingly tied round his neck. The Silvestre poetry is spoken, as it were, by one who stands to a certain degree outside himself, and who thus raises his writing to the 'contemplative plane' by offering his poetic situations for the comprehension of a reader who also stands outside them, and whose emotional reaction to them depends upon his having contemplated them, not identified himself with them; so that the satisfaction derived, both by the writer from producing the piece and by the reader from apprehending it, will come of resolving the situation into a form, not 'vibrating' with, or in response to, the feeling contained in it or overflowing from it. A slightly earlier and even better song than any of these Silvestre settings, *Les Berceaux* (words by Sully-Prudhomme, a poet whose sensibility, at least equal to Silvestre's, was complemented by a sense of design worthy of Leconte de Lisle) illustrates very much the same point. The poem is worth quoting in full:

Le long du quai, les grands vaisseaux
Que la houle incline en silence
Ne prennent pas garde aux berceaux
Que la main des femmes balance.

Mais viendra le jour des adieux
Car il faut que les femmes pleurent,
Et que les hommes curieux
Tentent les horizons qui leurrent!

Et ce jour-là les grands vaisseaux,
Fuyant le port qui diminue,
Sentent leur masse retenue
Par l'âme des lointains berceaux.[1]

For to an English reader this will immediately suggest Kingsley's *Three Fishers*, and by so doing will indicate how far Fauré had progressed from the ballad-type to which Kingsley's verses served as a text. The poem, with its significant comparison of a swaying boat to a rocking cradle, is allowed to tell its tale without any sentimental intrusion from the 'moaning' of the harbour-bar; and the 12-8 movement of the music, by comparison with that of *Le Pays des rêves*, has become all the more appropriately lulling by the fact that the crotchet-and-quaver pattern in the right hand and the vocal part is combined with one of almost continuous quavers in the left:

[1] Of which I offer the following translation—not of course for singing purposes:

The great boats down in the harbour
Swayed by the swelling tide
Pay little heed to the cradles
Rocked at the women's side.

But soon the day of departure
Shall come, and women must weep
While men set forward to venture
The lure of the unknown deep.

And then the great boats receding
From the harbour soon lost to sight
Shall feel that the distant cradles
Still hold them with unseen might.

The song as a whole conveys a desire to resolve feeling into form rather than to be affected by feeling in itself.

By now Fauré had completely found himself as a song-writer. *Les Roses d'Ispahan* (Leconte de Lisle) is a love-song redolent of the voluptuous Epicureanism of the oriental model followed by the words—two stanzas of which, implying a certain disturbance of the prevailing calm, were omitted by the composer; and *Nocturne* (Villiers de l'Isle-Adam) rather carries on the oriental atmosphere by using a scale in which the second and third degrees waver between flat and natural while the seventh is found as a chromatic semitone from the tonic only in harmonic combinations which leave very little of its 'leading-note' character—in the vocal line it is consistently flattened—the whole resembling the oriental songs produced by the Russian composers. *Clair de lune* (Verlaine) is unforgettable; in it we have an unrivalled evocation of that Rococo culture whose memory has never been quite lost in France—the figures of the old masked comedy, disporting themselves against the background of a Watteau *fête galante*—by means of a musical vocabulary which is all the more strongly evocative of the past in that it harks back to the procedures of an age much more archaic than that of Watteau:

for here, under Fauré's favourite signature of five flats (the relative minor this time) there are in a modern form the dominant harmony with a minor third (a), and the tritonic melody-passages (b), suggesting that fidelity to strict modal forms which even at the end of the Middle Ages had been replaced in part by *musica ficta*, while by an ironical twist the words 'sur le mode mineur' are set to the one passage in the whole work (c) which comes nearest to major tonality. By means of this discreet archaism (which serves at the same time as the vehicle of a profound originality[1]) Fauré has conveyed, almost more surely even than Debussy, the nostalgia lurking ever behind the frivolous exterior of Verlaine's pastoral figures, who 'seem to doubt the happiness they sing'.[2]

Another setting of Verlaine, *Spleen* ('Il pleure dans mon cœur'), is regarded by M. Koechlin as superior to the rather better-known Debussy song on the same words. I cannot share the opinion; Debussy seems to me to have more accurately caught the nameless and almost morbid *malaise* indicated in the text and represented in the title—though in fact the application of that title (whose French meaning has moved rather a long way from that of the English word whence it was borrowed) to that particular poem was Fauré's own doing, and not even Verlaine's; the *Spleen* of which John Ireland has set a translation is a different poem. But in the next two years (1890-91) Fauré went to Verlaine for the words of two groups of songs which show him at the height of his power: the five written in Venice (Op. 58) and *La Bonne Chanson* (Op. 61).

The 'cinq mélodies de Venise' left no doubt, if any had still existed, that a composer had arisen in whose name French song could hold its head high against any in the world. There is little of Venice about them except the accident of their having been

[1] As may also be said of the Balakirev group of composers in Russia and of Vaughan Williams in England.

[2] 'Ils n'ont pas l'air de croire à leur bonheur': the translation is by Arthur Symons.

written there—though one of them, *Mandoline* (also set by Debussy) is related, like *Clair de lune*, to the Italian masked comedy, and another, *A Clymène*, is set to Fauré's favourite barcarolle rhythm. Rather do they continue to translate into musical form that rarefied and yet voluptuous civilization of which the *fête galante* was the symbol, Watteau the prophet and Verlaine the later rhapsodist, and which so many Frenchmen—notably the novelist Henri de Régnier—were apt to detect, not only in Versailles where one can most readily believe it still to survive, but also in the city of the Carnival: that Carnival which, though for the Italians themselves it was probably never anything more recondite than a riotous saturnalia, has long appeared to the French imagination as the perfect frame for a life of moonlight confidences and subtle evasions, where the Masks and the Bergomasks 'feign indifference in the moments of their passion and passion in those of their indifference'[1] and where love-making itself lost half its *embarras* by losing all its *naïveté*.

These five songs are a cycle by almost as good a right as the *Bonne Chanson*; for their construction is cyclic in the Franck sense of a reappearance of themes from one to another. In one case it is almost a bodily transference of this passage from *En sourdine*:

to the last of the series, *C'est l'extase*, where it appears thus:

[1] Jankélévitch, *op. cit.*, p. 136.

the phrase carrying in both places a wonderful suggestion of retired restfulness through being built on that most tranquil of chords, the minor seventh. There is furthermore a thematic thread of a more fugitive kind running through all the five, which may be stated in its simplest form thus:

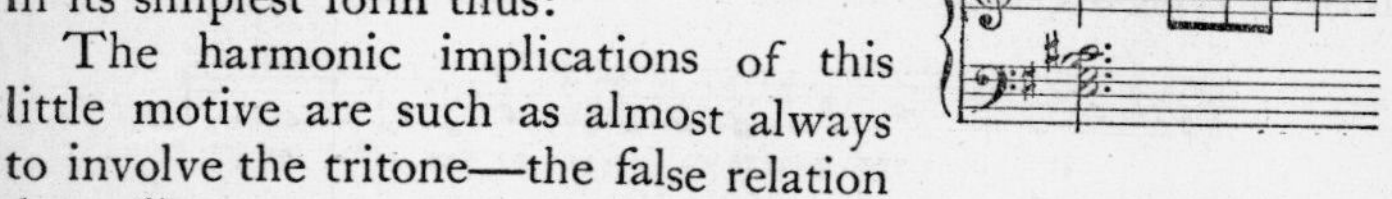

The harmonic implications of this little motive are such as almost always to involve the tritone—the false relation depending on an augmented fourth between successive notes in different parts of the texture; as will be readily understood by examining either of the following harmonies which at various places accompany it:

Here we have a Fauré 'finger-print' which has made the fortune of many compositions since; it served to raise the musical quality of certain passages in Puccini's *Madam Butterfly*:

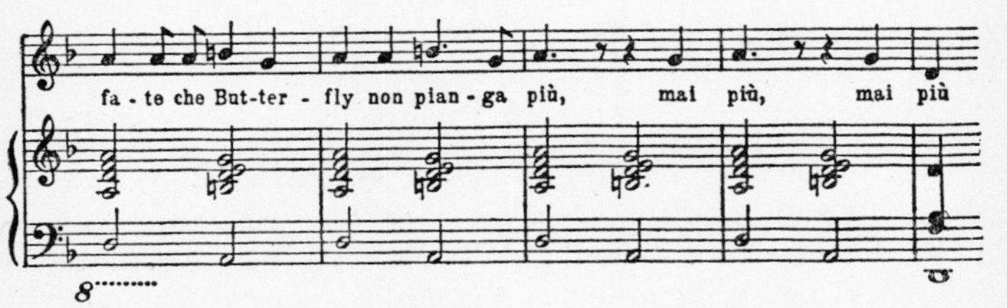

and had lost none of its effectiveness when Debussy used it to form a typical cadence in the *Noël des enfants*:

Its use in the *Mélodies de Venise* may be taken almost to typify that service which Fauré was all the more able to render to modern music because of the modal training he had undergone, and which consisted not so much in a revival of the 'Gregorian' modes themselves as in a development, made with unerring taste, of just those elements in the modal language which the medieval and Renaissance composers had for various reasons denied themselves. In this direction his work was as fruitful as that of Mussorgsky, which under this aspect—and indeed under no other—it somewhat resembled.

Under no other, certainly: Fauré was the opposite of a 'noble savage' in music; and his *Bonne Chanson* is the supreme example in musical history of a work, written to an amorous programme, which loses nothing and gains a great deal by its tone of exquisite urbanity and by the sense of design, rather than of passionate outpouring, that pervades it. The words are a selection of nine out of the collection of poems written by Verlaine to his fiancée during his brief period of happiness as a prospective bridegroom; and Fauré's music—already far removed from the typical love-music of romanticism in that it celebrates the joy of loving, not its despair—repeats the success of the *Vénitiennes* in that it is even better than its text. For Verlaine, keenly-armed and delicate poet though he was, sometimes lacks the last touch of reserve—the almost untranslatable French term for it is *pudeur*—which will enable an artist to endure the more penetrating scrutiny of a civilized mind. M. Jankélévitch has expressed this in terms upon which I cannot hope to improve, though I adapt some of his metaphors:

> This reserve, of which poor Lélian [Verlaine's anagrammatic name for himself] was deprived to an almost incredible degree by his weakness for absinthe, nevertheless envelops the *Bonne Chanson*, just as in the *Fêtes galantes* [*i.e.* in the collection of poems from which the words of *Clair de lune* and *Mandoline* were drawn] it accounted for the disproportion between ardent emotion and evasive language. . . . The *Mélodies de Venise* had stood for 'kisses light as air and feelings on the surface of our souls'; while on the other hand, now that he was fairly away on the wings of joy, Fauré did not allow his transports to get out of hand. . . . The *fêtes galantes* had been in their way serious, picnickings and minuets notwithstanding; and, conversely, there remains something light-hearted about the *Bonne Chanson*, despite the immense sweep of its joyous flight.[1]

Here, the construction is not only cyclic but almost symphonic. Fauré opens with the description of the Beloved as

[1] *Op. cit.*, pp. 136–7.

she first appears, something between a saint of legend and a great lady of feudal times—

> Une sainte en son auréole,
> Une châtelaine en sa tour

—set to a quiet triple movement, somewhat *archaïsant* here and there in its harmony:

which is followed immediately, in a way recalling the relation between the first two movements of Franck's Sonata, by a joyous *allegro*, a later fulfilment of the style previously employed for such happy love-songs as *Nell* and *Aurore*; in one place indeed the occurrence of the word *mousse* at the end of a line seems to have awoken in Fauré a memory of the phrases ending with the same word in *Les Roses d'Ispahan.*

The cycle continues through moods of deep peace (No. 3, the celebrated poem *L'heure exquise*, which is most familiar as the mere *romance de salon* that Reynaldo Hahn made of it, and at which Delius also tried his hand) or uncertainty, as in Nos. 4 and 5—the phrase 'des chemins perfides' is particularly well represented by one of Fauré's most deliciously devious progressions from and back to his tonality:

—or intimate and slightly troubled tenderness, represented by the rising and falling by means of augmented triads in *N'est-ce pas*, No. 8:

—or ambiguity, as when Verlaine prays that thoughts of him may visit the Beloved while she is still asleep, and at the same time salutes the dawn:

And it culminates in a final movement which gathers up and transforms thematic material from nearly all the others; the dawn-music of No. 6 has become the full tide of spring:

a phrase with a similar association from No. 2 is appropriated to the words '*every* season shall now be my delight', and the final apostrophe to Her, 'who is the glory of this ordered fantasy', repeats the music used to characterize her in No. 1.

La Bonne Chanson stands out pre-eminently even in Fauré's vocal writing for its serene resolution of feeling into form, the exact contrary of the kind of song which—as André Gide said of romantic art in general—is more concerned to afford evidence of emotion than to discover grounds for it.[1] Already it had been noticeable that the elegy on drowned sailors and their fellows who are more fortunate in a quieter rest, *Au Cimetière*, was more pathetic in its unstrained vocalization and its small melodic intervals, with Fauré's neo-modal harmonies to modify their apparent direction, than its companion piece, *Larmes*, where Richepin's direct invitation to the external signs of sorrow—'Pleurons nos chagrins, chacun le nôtre'—had been fitted by the composer with music bordering here and there on violence. The strenuous pathos of the Laocoön type, as M. Koechlin has remarked, was not the medium in which Fauré was most at home; he will not very readily invite us to be affected by the spectacle of feeling as such, but offers us rather a musical current whose flow is controlled by the purpose of artistic form, and beneath whose scarcely ruffled surface we may infer the very real depths indicated by his sinuous harmonic progressions. Verlaine's despair over his lost youth, represented by Fauré,

[1] 'L'important pour eux, n'est plus d'être mais de paraître ému.' (*Morceaux choisis*, p. 97.)

in *Prison* (Op. 83, No. 1) with an ascending series of recurrent chords of the eleventh dropping suddenly to a minor ninth, would lose rather than gain in poignancy if delivered with the sobbing accents of Italian *verismo.* And the three songs to words by Samain (*Arpège*, *Soir* and *Accompagnement*) carry to its farthest possible extent, by their essentially *contained* eloquence, the tendency of Fauré's songs at their best to sound like cross-sections through a timeless transfigured world.

Albert Samain's poetry is a continuation, so to speak, of Verlaine's; he displays the same sensitiveness to rare and distinguished forms of beauty, and the same disillusioned melancholy which in his own day was labelled 'decadent' by critics who preferred to suppose that this poetry was nothing but the dying fall of romantic aspirations. The difference between him and Verlaine is that Samain, while observing a greater discretion in the exposure of his inner world, frequently clothes his poetic statements in so extreme a language as almost to suggest the 'æsthetes' whom Gilbert parodied so unmercifully and, one must add, so uncomprehendingly. Fauré has tempered his poetry with the same sureness of touch as he previously applied to Verlaine. *Arpège* is a pastoral even further withdrawn into fantasy than *Clair de lune*, whose success it repeats; *Soir* is one of the most peaceful things I know in all music, the 'vaste et tendre apaisement' already celebrated in No. 3 of the *Bonne Chanson* being here, if anything, even more perfectly rendered by means of one of Fauré's most audacious enharmonic cadences in returning to his initial material:

while *Accompagnement*, though its words come near in places to caricaturing those of *Soir*—

> Trois grands lys frais coupés meurent sur mon manteau . . .
> Vers tes lèvres, ô nuit voluptueuse et pâle,
> Est-ce leur âme, est-ce mon âme qui s'exhale?[1]

—would redeem a far worse-proportioned text by its harmonic richness, the crowning moment of which is perhaps this chord of the thirteenth in which the minor ninth rises with a sense of fulfilment to its major[2]:

This and other excellences of Fauré's writing are combined in the *Forêt de septembre* (Catulle Mendès) where the 'Gregorian' touches that we saw in *Une Sainte* are found side by side with the flowing semiquaver movement of *Soir*, the whole moving

[1] Three lilies, newly plucked, droop on my cloak;
O pale voluptuous Night, is it their spirit
Or mine, that is out-breathed to meet thy kiss?

[2] This progression also is one of which later composers have made profitable use: Alfredo Casella employs it with the same 'peacefully expanding' effect in his *Siciliana* for pianoforte trio, as also does William Walton in the finale of his viola Concerto.

towards a succession of exquisite falling closes which leave an unsurpassed autumnal serenity in the listener's memory.

A serenity, moreover, which never degenerates into an attitudinizing solemnity. 'La sérénité n'est pas la lenteur', wrote Émile Vuillermoz with reference to *Pénélope*, and this is the key to the difference between Fauré's classic quietude and the long-drawn adagios of *Parsifal*. Fauré never drags; his style is as far removed as possible from that 'German andante' which someone described as 'the normal walking pace of a corpulent man', and which may be studied at will in the works of any of the lesser *Lieder* writers and even in some of those by the greater. His songs, like his pianoforte and chamber works, are essentially *movements* in the sense in which the term was applied in the eighteenth century—even when the mood they are to convey is one of stillness; in contrast with Delius, for whom rhythm itself will sometimes stand still[1], Fauré maintains an even but unflagging flow in his delivery of words[2], in his instrumental movement and in his harmonic progressions. The syllables of *Prison* are sung for the most part to a semiquaver division over a slow crotchet pulsation—the intimate tone of Verlaine's words, expressed by such familiar phraseology as 'toi que voilà', could not have been fittingly served by any wide-spaced declamation; the feature of a constant accompanying figure, set in the first bar and maintained throughout so as to carry an initial impetus uninterrupted to the end, may be found in almost any of Fauré's best songs, and not least significantly in *Le plus doux chemin*, a tiny 'madrigal'[3] whose words are from his old source,

[1] In the *Song of the High Hills*, for example.

[2] Without falling into the error of supposing that song is merely an 'extension' of speech, it is worth noticing that Fauré, among his other services to the French *mélodie*, put an end to the 'over-lengthened or over-shortened syllables' as well as to the 'infelicitous pauses' and 'telescopings' of phrases in the text, which so frequently marred the work of his predecessors. (Louis Vuillemin, *Gabriel Fauré et son œuvre*, p. 24).

[3] Not only does the word *madrigal*, for a Frenchman, not necessarily indicate a polyphonic composition as it did for our own 'madrigalists'; it normally describes, as it did for Molière and Boileau, a much more

Armand Silvestre, and of which Mr. Aaron Copland has said that 'all of Fauré is contained in its three short pages'[1]; while the characteristically 'soluble' harmonies are perhaps represented at their best in *Le Parfum impérissable*, a meditative setting of a sonnet by Leconte de Lisle, which might serve as a motto for Fauré's collected works, as indeed its title regularly does in the hands of most of his critics.[2] And rightly; for these verses, in which Leconte performed the wellnigh impossible feat of writing about hopeless love without exhibitionism or loss of dignity—this is due mainly, perhaps, to the fact that the passion of the subject is resolved into form by being presented under a comparison with the undying perfume of an eastern flower—are provided with music which should survive any change of fashion or evolution of technique, and which has even overcome its initial handicap of being dedicated to Paolo Tosti! It would be unfair to the whole song to quote any one or two bars from it; but the typically *unimpeded* character of Fauré's songs, which I have in this paragraph been analysing, may be very well represented under all its three aspects at once—easy flow of words, consistency of figuration and solubility of harmony—by this passage from *La Rose* (words also by Leconte de Lisle), a work of earlier date than those recently mentioned but belonging essentially to the same phase of its composer's development[3]; it is marked *andante* but displays a quite Mozartian reluctance towards any sagging into an *adagio*:

---

light-hearted, indeed frivolous production than we associate with the Elizabethan writers, many of whose madrigals are set to texts of a very wide lyric sweep and sometimes even of a certain philosophic pretension. The Fauré-Silvestre 'madrigal' on the other hand might be sung by a Louis XV courtier in a *fête galante*.

[1] *The Musical Quarterly* (New York), October 1924.

[2] *E.g.* Jean Chantavoine's obituary notice in the *Ménestrel*, 14th November 1924.

[3] Fauré appears to have revised the ending of *La Rose* between its appearance in the second *Recueil* and its transference to the third; in its later form the vocal line ends on a tonic F instead of a rhetorical high A and the cadence leading to this—originally depending simply

Fauré himself was evidently very much aware of this quality in his work, and of the unwillingness many singers would display to match the quality by their performance. To Mme. Baugnies (dedicatee of his first Nocturne) he once wrote with regard to *Green* (No 3. of the *Vénitiennes*): 'I cannot too strongly recommend you not to sing it slowly; its pace is almost breathless'[1]; and one gathers that this advice was given, not so much from a fear that she had mistaken the mood of the song, as from a suspicion that she might not wish to proceed at the pace he had himself imagined through a scheme in which a harmony is no sooner established than it resolves into another. It was doubtless for a very similar reason that Saint-Saëns, his loyal and lifelong supporter, confessed that he could make nothing of the *Bonne Chanson* when it appeared—though afterwards he recanted handsomely.[2] And it is only too probable that the average French singer of Fauré's time, brought up almost exclusively on nineteenth-century opera, found the intervals of his songs as unexpected and as difficult to manage as many of our English singers, brought up with equal exclusiveness on the restricted range of intervals and of harmony in all but the very greatest of the *Lieder*, still do.

---

on a major ninth over the tonic bass, a chord which he had made his own from very early days—now takes a slightly more devious route by introducing the major seventh with minor third, a chord closely allied to those augmented triads which were to be the main modulatory instrument of his final period.

[1] Quoted by P. Fauré-Fremiet, *op. cit.*, p. 52.

[2] P. Fauré-Fremiet, *op. cit.*, p. 37.

One need not suppose this executant incapacity to have been the reason, but it is a fact that the last phase of Fauré's production in song-form is marked by a much closer correspondence than previously between the vocal line and the pianoforte part. *Arpège* is the last song in which he used the device of a counter-melody interwoven with the melody in the voice-part, and even there it is not as continuous as in *Clair de lune*, but is introduced with a thematic rather than what Debussy would have called an 'arabesque' significance.[1] Of course the 'soloist's prestige' of the vocal line was not at any stage of Fauré's writing such as to justify a use of the term 'accompaniment' in the old 'vassal' sense; Philippe Fauré-Fremiet remarks with regard to the *Vénitiennes* and the *Bonne Chanson*[2] that 'it was no longer a question of melody and accompaniment, but of a musical structure whose basic idea is more apparent in the harmonic movement than in the melodic line itself'. Which is not a subtraction of interest from the voice-part, but rather an addition, by enabling the voice to share in other features of musical interest besides the purely melodic one. This is what happened in *Le Parfum impérissable*; and it may also be observed in other songs of the same period—consider this passage from *La Fleur qui va sur l'eau*:

The texture of Fauré's writing is becoming at once simpler and more individual; not that his songs, from Op. 18 onwards at any rate, could ever have been mistaken for another composer's,

[1] Readers of Mr. E. Lockspeiser's *Debussy* in this series will remember how a 'musical arabesque, or principle of ornament', was detected by Debussy as a basic principle of art both in Bach and in the sixteenth-century polyphonists (p. 220).

[2] *Op. cit.*, p. 52.

but it is as though the simplification of his designs had obliged each 'curve' and 'surface' in them to take on an intensified significance because the reduced number of the elements has extended the function of each. On these lines Fauré produced in 1907 *La Chanson d'Ève*, an album of ten songs in which, after giving out a plainchant-like phrase derived from Mélisande's song, by way of motto to the series:

and following it up in the first song by passages of this kind, the nearest that he came to complication in the whole work:

he continued in somewhat the manner of *Soir* (and in the same key of D flat—No 5) but with a much more rapid succession of harmonic suspensions:

and completed the set with a structurally bare but harmonically tortuous piece of tone-weaving:

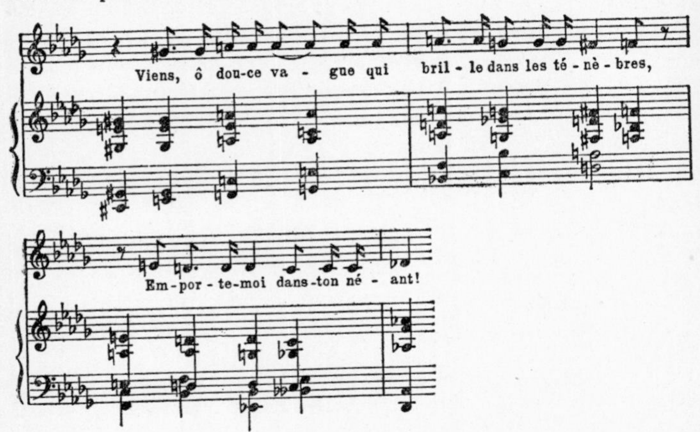

which was a favourite pattern of these later years, since it is followed in *Le Jardin clos* for No. 5 (*Dans la Nymphée*) and, not quite so closely, for No. 8 (*Inscription sur le sable*) and reappears in the incomparable *Diane, Séléné* of his last volume, published in 1922.

The text of the *Chanson d'Ève* is a group of poems of a pantheistic turn by Charles van Lerberghe (a Belgian poet known chiefly, indeed, by a drama called *Pan*) in which 'la jeune et divine Ève' contemplates and interprets the newly-created world in a way suggesting Paul Valéry's *Jeune Parque*, though without his symbolistic obscurity; the affinity of Van Lerberghe's poetry is rather with Baudelaire and his aim to make 'perfumes, colours and sounds correspond to each other'—as when, in the seventh poem of the group, Eve asks if the Adam whom she has not yet seen 'knows that my voice, still unheard by him, is imbued with the scent of my lilies'. This poetry, not obscure in expression but difficult to pin down to a circumscribed meaning, evidently provided for Fauré the same attraction of the unsubstantial which some others, endowed with a less alert sense of literary criticism, found in Maeterlinck[1]; and it represents the same development out of Verlaine and Samain as is manifested by Fauré's music for it in relation to that which he provided for those two poets. Plainly he found the collaboration congenial, for he drew on Van Lerberghe again for his next volume of songs, *Le Jardin clos*, which has a great deal in common with its predecessor. A little too much in common, Mr. Copland considered; he found in it 'a regrettable tendency to repeat certain mannerisms'.[2] It is true that in these songs Fauré relies more and more, for the purposes of harmonic progression, either on the augmented triad (which had been his constant resource in *Pénélope*) or on passages of this 'anticipated' or 'suspended' kind:

and that his method of enharmonics and passing-notes is here strained to its utmost limits:

[1] For whose curious mixture of the ponderous and the childish (Romain Rolland called him 'part sublime, part silly') Fauré had so little use, in spite of having written incidental music for *Pelléas et Mélisande*, that he once parodied the Maeterlinck manner in a mock ballad, *Les trois fils du roi sourd*. (P. Fauré-Fremiet, *op. cit.*, pl. XLIV).

[2] *Loc. cit.*, *supra*.

But I do not think this detracts any more essentially from the value of these compositions than do Elgar's rising and falling sevenths, Brahms's fondness for an anticipated heavy beat or the consecutive triads of Vaughan Williams. At any rate there is nothing otiose in this use of another of Fauré's regular resources, the unprepared major seventh, in a passage from one of his next book of four songs, *Mirages* (No. 3):

nor in the rest of the same series; the long sinuous monologue of *Reflets dans l'eau* is like the surface of water itself in its effortless fluidity, while all critics combine to acclaim *Danseuse* as one of the most vertiginous things ever written—and that without the aid of dynamics or acrobatics.

Fauré's last *opus* for voice and pianoforte, *L'Horizon chimérique*, constitutes a wonderful farewell to this branch of his art. The words are by a young man killed in the 1914 war, Jean de la Ville de Mirmont (son of a Bordeaux University professor), who in these four poems did a thing unusual with French poets, for he treated of the sea as primarily a symbol of the undiscovered, not as a source of human tragedy like Richepin, Corbière or Pierre Loti, and thus gave a new lease of life to what Mr. T. S. Eliot (quoting perhaps another writer? I do not know) described as 'la poésie des départs'.[1] One thinks immediately of the Duparc-Baudelaire *Invitation au voyage*; and then one realizes the difference: Duparc's song, like Baudelaire's words, is an exotic, while *L'Horizon chimérique* is an exercise not so much of the imagination as of the unusually awakened consciousness. The effect of this dead young man's poetry set to music by an old man of seventy-seven, as Fauré now was, is to sound at the same time like a farewell to life and like a readiness to encounter whatever lies beyond death—

> My dreams shall bear them company,
> Ships in whose wake my heart long since has followed.[2]

—a readiness tempered somewhat by a longing after the 'lovely gifts of shade, and slumber, and deep peace'[3] represented by the one 'nocturne' in a book of 'marine landscapes', the exquisite *Diane, Séléné*, which I will not trust myself to praise any further. Instead, having fairly launched out on a sea of quotation, I may perhaps be forgiven for drawing at some length upon M. Jankélévitch, if only to show what can be done in the way of criticism by means of a paragraph consisting chiefly of reminiscences of the titles of Fauré's and other composers' works:

> The Africa of which Chausson dreamed existed only in his imagination, and Duparc also, haunted as he was by fabulous shores, welcomed an *invitation to travels* on which he knew he would never set forth. It will be objected that Fauré also felt a longing for some *horizon chimérique* [I shall not attempt to translate this title], and that the adventures that he hoped to meet therein were nothing but fresh *mirages*, nothing but *reflections in the water*. This, in a way, is true; and yet, whereas the romantics thought they were escaping and in fact were merely sounding the

[1] *Baudelaire*, in *Selected Essays*, p. 377.

[2] '. . . ils feront une escorte
Aux vaisseaux que mon cœur dans leur fuite à suivis'.

[3] Clemence Dane, *Will Shakespeare*, Act I.

> depths of their own souls for some *memory of a previous existence*[1], Fauré looks fearlessly out beyond him; his new worlds may be unsubstantial, but they are not imaginary.[2]

No one, I think, has ever felt impelled to describe Fauré's music as 'dreamy'; it is *abstracted*, which is a very different thing. The romantic identification of the ideal with the unreal was quite foreign to him, and his inner consciousness, however much intensified, felt no repugnance towards externalizing itself.

Looking back over Fauré's hundred songs one is impressed chiefly, I think, with the fact that they combine a high level of musical achievement with an unusual sensitiveness to the quality of their words. Musical they are in the highest sense, making as they do hardly any concessions to the tricks of vocalism or to the appeal of the human voice as an instrument for obtaining, as M. Jean Cocteau put it, emotional results by sentimental blackmail.[3] And of Fauré's success in partnership with fine poetry it is not too much to say, with M. Jean Chantavoine:

> By his songs he sealed the reconciliation of poetry and music, romanticism having made rivals of them and the art of the classical age having subordinated the latter to the former.[4]

Even those among the romantic poets who responded most readily to music were liable for the most part to produce poetry quite unsuitable for musical setting, because its own pattern of sonorities was too obtrusive—we have already considered in this connexion the case of Victor Hugo, and that of Browning in England may serve as a parallel—and it is not surprising that Fauré's triumphs were scored with the help of those poets who represent not the sonorous but the evocative power of words: what the French rather untranslatably call *le verbe*. This term,

[1] 'La réminiscence d'une vie antérieure', *cf.* the Duparc title.
[2] *Op. cit.*, p. 225.
[3] *Le Coq et l'Arlequin*, in *Le Rappel á l'Ordre*, p. 19.
[4] In the *Ménestrel* for 13th June 1922.

PAGE OF MANUSCRIPT OF THE C MINOR QUARTET

originally of course bearing the theological sense of 'the Word', the medium of divine revelation, is now currently employed to indicate 'language in its poetic function', *i.e.* as conveying a fuller meaning than that carried by words in their ordinary use—sometimes even an occult meaning. And we may agree with M. Chantavoine that Fauré, the revealer of unexpected significances in sounds, was the perfect partner for those *poètes du verbe*—Leconte de Lisle, Sully-Prudhomme, Verlaine, Samain—who in the 'Parnassian' and 'Symbolist' periods of French poetry helped their readers to discover those meanings, latent in words, which the emphatic methods of romanticism had left unheard amidst the clamour:

> It is not enough to say that he was their *interpreter*, nor even their *complement*. . . . In some cases he has actually *revealed* them, by opening up for them that region of our minds which the choicest words in poetic speech have otherwise failed to penetrate. . . . In this respect Gabriel Fauré (together with Henri Duparc) played, in the Parnassian and Symbolist age of France, a part recalling that of Schumann in the romantic age of Germany; on this account he belongs henceforth, not merely to the history of French music, but to that of French poetry and French artistic sensibility.[1]

[1] J. Chantavoine, obituary article in the *Ménestrel*, 14th November 1924.

CHAPTER V

THE CHAMBER MUSIC

IN chamber music Fauré found himself with real completeness at an earlier date than in any other branch of his art. The violin Sonata, Op. 13, and the pianoforte Quartet, Op. 15, may fairly be described as works of his maturity; and indeed when they appeared, in 1876 and 1879 respectively, he was already over thirty years old—but his was not the precocious type of genius, and one has to wait some time before coming upon anything of such sustained excellence in other departments of his writing. In the pianoforte works, for example, there is little that we can regard as having completely emerged from the stage of apprenticeship—except perhaps the *Ballade*—until half a dozen years later; which may be explained in part by the nature of the models available to Fauré's hand. The reaction against the eighteenth century had played greater havoc with pianoforte solo than with chamber music, no doubt because of the greater accessibility of the medium. But even in the less vulgarized domain of the chamber ensemble it is remarkable that a work displaying the specific virtues of the Sonata should have been produced at so early a date. Brahms, who as H. C. Colles remarked was the only composer writing first-rate chamber works during the third quarter of the century, was virtually unknown in France at the time—which is just as well, for it would have done Fauré no good to be influenced by him, even supposing he had been amenable to it; and as for César Franck's Sonata, apparent resemblances notwithstanding (I think they are mostly due to similarity of key), it was written ten years later than Fauré's, a fact which impelled M. Charles Koechlin to demand that we should 'render unto Gabriel the things which are Gabriel's, and not unto César'.[1]

It is appropriate, therefore, that the qualities most noticeable in Fauré's chamber works should from the earliest be those of his own originality. Foremost among them I would place a

[1] Koechlin, *Gabriel Fauré*, p. 106.

certain irresistible rhythmic impetus in which he reminds us of the eighteenth-century masters by his power of maintaining the flow of a movement, at whatever speed, without falling into monotony. His unwillingness to waste time over 'introductions' of the Lisztian kind has often been remarked upon; the most he ever does in this way is a bar or two to establish the rhythm, as in the finale of the Sonata Op. 13 or the first movement of the Quartet Op. 45. And this is characteristic; for not only is a Fauré movement set going without any elaborate preparation, but it is not held up *en route*; the dramatic pauses of Franck, and even the sudden outbursts of Beethoven, let alone the rhetorical devices which make so much of Liszt's music sound like 'introductions to introductions'[1], are equally foreign to Fauré's method. The rhythm of his movements is part of their design, and is in no sense a reflexion of the necessarily interrupted rhythm of events outside. He establishes a rhythmic unit in the earliest bars of a movement, *e.g.* the first of the Sonata:

or the first of the Quartet Op. 15:

which throughout the rest of the piece will seldom be absent from the design; that of the Quartet even appears in the development section simultaneously with its own second subject. The

[1] See Tovey, *Essays in Musical Analysis*, Vol. II, p. 7.

consistency of figuration in the pianoforte part helps to the same end; throughout Fauré's chamber works, by a process which was to culminate in the great second Quintet of 1921, an important function of the pianoforte writing is the maintenance of an irresistible rhythmic unity, in the same way as it was on a smaller scale in the accompaniments to his songs. And moreover this is accomplished without inviting the suggestion, occasionally aroused by the figuration in Schubert or Mendelssohn, that the pianist's hands are busy to no purpose. Fauré's pianoforte parts do not, as the French express it, beat against the void; and in this respect he has escaped, more successfully than any of the romantic composers, the pitfall corresponding in the nineteenth century to that which in the eighteenth awaited all users of the Alberti bass. He had a very accurate sense of what was appropriate to the design of his works from among the various possibilities of development latent in his thematic material; where Dvořák and even Brahms will sometimes leave the impression that a piece of working-out has been done merely because it was technically feasible, Fauré maintains his faculty for development in subordination to his sense of significant form. And this along with a freer sense of the 'responsibilities' of themes than the academically established principle of thematic contrast would allow for; even the faithful M. Koechlin finds it necessary almost to apologize for his frequent metamorphosis of a 'masculine theme' into a 'kind of distant evocation',[1] as in the Quartet Op. 15, where the vigorous melody quoted above appears at the end of the exposition in the following form:

[1] Koechlin, *op. cit.*, p. 107.

Evidently Fauré did not envisage the sonata form as indissolubly bound up with any principle of contrasted themes such as the textbooks used to describe as 'masculine and feminine subjects'; and certainly his second subjects are not delivered with the air of beginning a new chapter, but appear as it were without 'announcement' and without any break in the consistent flow of a movement. And the rhythmic pervasiveness of his first subjects is attended with such remarkable transformations of their mood that these movements are an unrivalled model of diversity in unity. The opening *allegro* of the second pianoforte Quartet, Op. 45, may serve here as an even better example than that of the first; for the 'forging' theme[1] with which it opens not only appears as a 'falling close' in the codetta to the exposition, but is modified to a quieter mood in the next section as follows, with the pianoforte part in a kind of augmentation:

while between the two Fauré has inserted, in the same way in which Mozart used to begin his development sections, an entirely new motive:

[1] The rhythm of this subject is said by Fauré's biographers to have been a reminiscence of the noise made by an iron-works, driven by

which (again like its Mozartian counterpart) assumes great importance as the movement progresses.

In the matter of structural outlines Fauré was not an innovator; for the most part he was content to take the sonata form as he found it—except that during his final period he tended either to eliminate the scherzo or to fuse it with the finale, a matter which will be discussed in its place. Neither was he much attracted to the cyclic form with which the name of Franck is so closely identified. There is only one example in his chamber works of this kind of thematic transference—the scherzo of the Quartet Op. 45—and it is a notable one; more notable than one would gather, for example, from Mr. Aaron Copland's description[1]:

> The scherzo breaks away from the traditional minuet-form long enough to bring back a fragment of the opening theme of the first movement in a most refreshing manner.

or even from Philippe Fauré's:

> Once only, in the second Quartet, he transferred a motive from the opening *allegro* to the scherzo which followed it.[2]

In fact *both* subjects of the first movement are quoted in the scherzo, modified in their transition from 4-4 to 6-8 time; and not merely quoted, for they form the entire thematic material of the movement except for the opening *lezghinka*-like motive.[3] In general, however, Fauré relied, consciously or otherwise, upon his own sense of musical architecture to guide him through

---

water-power from a fast mountain stream at Montgauzy, where he lived between the ages of four and nine. (Koechlin, *op. cit.*, p. 6, n., and elsewhere.)

[1] *The Musical Quarterly* (New York), October 1924.

[2] P. Fauré-Fremiet, *Gabriel Fauré*, p. 31.

[3] There is in fact one more example, but it really is in this case a momentary and not a 'cyclic' transference: in the second violin Sonata a phrase from the opening 9-4 movement is quoted, in a transformed 2-2 shape, towards the end of the finale.

the traditional sonata-form as the nineteenth century had received it from the Viennese masters; and this sense very seldom betrayed him. He was able to write movements of considerable length without their appearing tediously drawn out, and to build up a climax without spoiling it by the suggestion of a series of minor climaxes leading to it, as sometimes happens for example in the less successful pages of Dvořák. This no doubt is partly due to his harmonic originality; in music whose phrases are not given to ending on a six-four chord, and which seldom seeks to draw attention to its outlines by perfect cadences, there is no inducement to take either the one or the other as the signal for a rhetorical peroration.

As with the whole designs, so with the single strokes that go to make them. Fauré does not disdain to use some of the traditional means of developing a theme; but he does not use them in such a way as to suggest that he had lost sight of the relation between the parts and the whole. A leading example of what I mean is to be found in his treatment of the device of doubled phrases—as it were the parallelism of the Psalms, except that in its more usual form it consists in an identical, not an approximate, repetition. This procedure, which grew up as a measure of symmetry in the Italo-German tradition of the eighteenth century and 'crystallized out' into a mere habit at the beginning of the nineteenth, was employed, by those romantic composers who prided themselves on not being strangers to the academic forms (but who mostly used them quite uncritically), as a means either of achieving length or of driving in their statements by sententious emphasis. The merest small change of music is thus regularly found twice over in the general run of nineteenth-century composition, while any phrase of greater importance is liable—even by the major composers of the period—to be 'hammered' or 'rubbed in' according to a formula for which Beethoven himself cannot altogether escape responsibility. Fauré accepts the formula, more or less, in the finale of the first Quartet—though even here his repetitions are neither otiose nor emphatic; in the Sonata Op. 13 it is modified by distribution between the parts:

in the *adagio* of the second Quartet the doubled phrases are no longer identical, but the second is made to lead necessarily forward to some further statement (since one vice of the musical parallelism here discussed, besides the danger of emphasis, is that it is liable to convey an impression of 'marking time on the spot', quite at variance with the sense of unimpeded movement so characteristic of Fauré's music in the main):

while elsewhere the repeated phrase embodies so significant a movement *within itself* (usually an harmonic progression of particular savour) as to invest the repetition with an oscillatory motion like that of a shuttle:

which produces a delicious 'rocking' effect:

and was to recur in one of the loveliest passages of his Trio:

*D

Sometimes it is as though he cannot bear to part at once with some particularly fine piece of inventive eloquence:

and lastly, to match the increasing importance of sequential treatment in his work, we find the latter part of a repeated phrase varied in such a manner as to lead into the sequence[1] —a device appearing already in the second Quartet but exemplified with especial aptness in this passage from the first Quintet, Op. 89 (see opposite page).

The same sureness of taste which is essential in order to decide which are the phrases that can bear, and indeed almost call for, repetition (but not for repetitiveness) is also indispensable in the selection of material appropriate for sequential use; and Fauré, who was as fond of sequences as Elgar, had this sureness of taste in at least as high a degree as his English contemporary, so that his sequential writing is as seldom tedious as his repetitions are seldom redundant. His style tended towards proportion and concision at a time when the musical models most widely followed—even Wagner—were rather given, like Browning's thrush, to singing everything twice over. And his avoidance of this vice has even acted as a bar to his appreciation among those on whom the other models had imposed themselves; M. Koechlin has noted how not only the chamber music but even the songs, because they do not express themselves in an insistent manner, will 'disconcert those elementary intelligences who expect us to emphasize and to repeat ourselves.'[2]

[1] The quotation on p. 163 from the Prelude to *Pelléas* illustrates the same feature.

[2] Koechlin, *op. cit.*, p. 200.

These and similar matters, such as the predominance of harmonic over dynamic interest in the texture of his works, indicate perhaps that Fauré's music in some respects carried on a chamber tradition more strongly rooted in the eighteenth century than that of the avowedly post-Beethovenian writers ever was. Nowhere is this more evident than in his slow movements, which

are neither the introspective Beethoven *adagio* nor the guileless Schubert *andantino*; for whereas the former of these proceeds with a lingering motion such as might have been the composer's own on his favourite country walks, and the latter is inclined to amble, a Fauré *andante* is more literally a *movement* than either. The consistent rhythmic figuration of the pianoforte part, which is as distinctive a feature of these as of the faster movements, at once invites a comparison with those eighteenth-century andantes where, though the beat was slow, the passage-work gave anything but a dragging effect[1]—a feature which may also be observed in those composers of the early nineteenth century, such as Hummel and up to a point Mendelssohn, who, either literally or by the allegiance of their practice, were pupils of Haydn and Mozart rather than of Beethoven and Schubert, and whose chamber works had (in so far as any chamber work had at that time) a greater vogue in France than people outside the country sometimes remember.

Even the impact of Schumann on this tradition had, for the most part, merely the effect of encouraging it along its own most distinctive lines with a somewhat richer harmony; so that Fauré may be said in a sense to have been the only composer who carried on from Schumann in a different direction from that followed by Brahms. It is notable indeed that in his earliest chamber work there is one point at which he takes after Schumann more patently than he was ever to do again; for the trio of the scherzo in the Sonata Op. 13 is in almost every respect like a Schumann 'intermezzo' section, and is unique in Fauré's work by the *contrast* that it presents with the scherzo proper. The corresponding portion of the Quartet Op. 15 is far more a *continuation* of what has preceded it—the rhythm is scarcely slackened, the time-signature remains constant, and the figuration is almost identical; and in Fauré's other scherzos (those of the Quartet Op. 45 and the second Quintet Op. 115) there is nothing that can be called a trio-section at all, for his principle of rhythmic consistency throughout a movement has triumphed here as elsewhere.

All these scherzos would in any case be remarkable for their feathery lightness, unsurpassed even by the fairy music of Mendelssohn; but I wish more particularly to adduce them here, along with the whole works to which they belong, as evidence that in his chamber music Fauré eliminates from his background,

[1] Is it not to a comprehension of this fact about eighteenth-century music that Prokofiev owes some of the success of the slow movement in his 'Classical Symphony'?

to a great degree, what we are accustomed to regard as the distinctive contribution of the nineteenth century. In this form of composition, which perhaps had suffered less than some others at the hands of those reformers to whom 'tone-poems' meant something different from tone-architecture, he found full scope for a musical rather than a sentimental sensibility. And his chamber works seem to announce themselves as the work of one who had taken up a thread, not exactly from where Mozart and his contemporaries had left it, but from where he would have found it had they been able to hand it on—had music in the nineteenth century not been deflected in so many ways from the evolution pointed out to it by the eighteenth. Fauré's greater familiarity, as a Frenchman, with a phase of composition which never quite got itself accepted as a main line of development must, I think, have helped him to this end; to use another metaphor, it is as though he had been able to proceed from the farther side of a gap which had never quite been bridged.

The fact that he was not very readily at home with the orchestra serves, if anything, to increase his appositeness for chamber composition. To venture for a moment on the hazardous comparison of music with painting, he was not to any great extent a composer in 'colour', if by colour in music we agree to denote the characteristics of instrumental *timbre*; one or two exceptions notwithstanding, such as the melody at the beginning of the *adagio* in Op. 45, of which M. Koechlin said that the viola would have had to be invented for it did the instrument not exist already[1], it does not appear that the peculiar qualities of instruments in any great measure dictated the music he wrote for them. I am careful to specify this meaning of 'colour' because to describe Fauré as 'mainly a composer in *line*' might easily involve an injustice to one of the greatest *harmonists* in the history of music. The comparison must be pursued farther; the corresponding element to harmony in painting is not colour but *mass*, such as we find it in the work of those painters who were not primarily colourists—Cézanne, for example—and in whose pictures it is as likely as not to arise out of the intersection

[1] *Op. cit.*, p. 107.

of lines and planes, just as Fauré's harmony derived in great measure from his linear counterpoint. Herein lies the difference between his harmonic significance and Debussy's; his contribution to the future of harmony was as vital as the younger composer's, but whereas Debussy approached compound sonorities as the primary material of his art, Fauré's harmonic enterprise has always a 'linear' reference. One may suppose that his original inclinations this way were confirmed by his training at the Niedermeyer under Saint-Saëns, who shared to the full the admiration of the school for Bach; for it is equally a distinguishing mark of Bach's music that his skill in the interweaving of linear parts helped him to his position in the forefront of harmonic originality.

The remark of M. Émile Vuillermoz, his pupil, that Fauré 'concealed his harmonic learning where another composer would have advertised it'[1], serves to remind us of the transparency of texture which with him existed *together* with this pioneer significance, in a way to which there have been few parallels in music. It is a transparency, moreover, which has deceived some otherwise penetrating critics as to the real substance of his work. Mr. Kaikhosru Sorabji, whose own nationality tempts us to classify as 'oriental' his fondness for sheer difficulty of disentanglement in musical design, is perhaps the most notable of those who are thus misled into supposing that there is no 'body' in Fauré's productions. Mr. Sorabji's ideal in this respect is Reger, who indeed, by his alternation of monumental intricacies with *schlichte Weisen* whose innocence becomes positively embarrassing, may fairly be quoted as an example of all that Fauré was not; but even in Brahms it is apparently an attraction to many people that his 'wrestlings with the angel' should be so patently displayed. They are inclined to assume that where no strivings are apparent nothing has been achieved; and they tend to overlook any original work in art which is presented to them with an air, not of having discovered a new country, but of having known all the time that it was there. The

[1] In *Musica* for February 1909; quoted by Séré, *Musiciens français d'aujourd'hui*, p. 191.

misapprehension is one that goes down very deeply into the psychology of art, for it is due ultimately to the false value so often set on strenuousness, as such. From this error, partly romantic and partly what Matthew Arnold would have called Hebraic[1], derived in great part the fortunes of German music in the nineteenth century; through accepting it, not only in this country but in some departments of French musical life itself, it became possible to identify 'depth' in art with those uneasy stirrings which so often are nothing but turgidity, and to treat as superficial the 'Olympian' serenity of those artists who had, as it were, no need to wrestle with the angel, but had him at their service from the first. The common valuation of Beethoven above Mozart, from which to this day we have not entirely recovered, was symptomatic of the same critical vice; a vice which was erected into a system by such writers as Adolf Weissmann, according to whom (as Professor Dent compendiously explained him) no art could be of the first order unless it were *problematisch*—*i.e.*, not 'problematic' in our sense, but contributory, on some ground other than the æsthetic one, to the solution of a problem. Such a view of art would hold little appeal for anyone who had heeded the advice of Beethoven's greatest German contemporary, 'that a production will give us all the more pleasure in that it has come readily and with ease to the artist'[2]; and Fauré, who had solved (or *resolved*) his material far too completely for his music ever to sound 'uncomfortable', answers so appositely to this description—originally intended by Goethe for the art of classical Greece—that we may fairly apply to his work in general the words used by Mr. Copland for the *adagio* of his pianoforte Quartet Op. 45: 'Its beauty is a truly classic one if we define classicism as "intensity on a background of calm".'[3]

[1] In *Culture and Anarchy*: with reference especially to the outlook of the Old Testament prophets on life, as consisting mainly in arduous duties to be fulfilled rather than (as for the Hellenes) in opportunities of comprehension to be grasped.

[2] Goethe, *Antik und modern*.

[3] *Loc. cit., supra.*

There are various pieces on a smaller scale which very well illustrate his power, shared with the greatest classic masters, of treating a slight subject in such a way as not to appear at all restricted by its slightness. The *Berceuse*, perhaps the least distinguished of them—it answered the demand of his publisher Hamelle for something to balance the possibility of a financial loss on the first Quartet—is nevertheless not altogether unworthy; the *Andante*, printed as Op. 75 but probably written earlier than this would imply, begins innocently enough, but conveys a pleasant sense of being carried along by the impetus of its own invention, so that it does not need to resort to conventional means of rounding off its phrases; while the *Fantaisie* for flute and piano, written as a Conservatoire competition piece, exploits all the resources of the flute without ever degenerating into mere virtuosity. Especially notable are Fauré's contributions to the repertory of the violoncello; the *Sicilienne*, dedicated to W. H. Squire[1], is one of the few works of his which occasionally found their way into 'celebrity' concerts of the familiar type, whereas the *Sérénade* Op. 98 is hardly heard at all, and the *Élégie*, though it penetrated as far as the gramophone catalogues, has been welcomed as a concert piece only by those cellists who are prepared to devote intellectual as well as technical attention to the works they perform. For, though it derives essentially from the kind of music represented by Massenet's *Élégie*, it is so far 'sublimated' from it as to be (what Massenet's music never was) inaccessible to the sentimentalist, and has a good title to be considered the finest single piece for violoncello and piano outside the range of sonata form.

Apart from a few of these minor productions, Fauré wrote between 1886 and 1916 only one chamber work, planned (and announced for publication) as early as 1890 but not issued until 1906, and even then perhaps only because the New York publisher Schirmer had pressed for its completion. This was the first pianoforte Quintet, Op. 89, dedicated to Eugène Ysaÿe (to whom so many French composers have been indebted for the

[1] And afterwards inserted into the *Pelléas et Mélisande* incidental music.

public presentation of their chamber music), originally intended to be a quartet like its two predecessors, and returned many times to the stocks before its composer would give it the *imprimatur.* Florent Schmitt's description of it as 'perhaps a rather hurriedly written work'[1] is therefore evidently misapplied, unless he merely meant that it was hurriedly *completed.* Whether he was justified in remarking that it is 'inferior to the quartets in thematic invention' is also a question which, to my mind, cannot be answered at all simply. The opening theme at any rate is one of Fauré's most characteristic, being cast in D minor with frequent B naturals, so that, as Vincent d'Indy remarked[2], it shows the unmistakable influence of the first Gregorian mode:

the second subject, where not only the sixth but also the second and fourth degrees of the scale waver between the smaller and the larger interval, has all the evanescent grace that we associate with Fauré in his best-known mood—and in fact bears some resemblance to the cyclic motive of the Venetian songs written only recently before it:

while Mr. Copland has remarked upon the technical mastery with which 'the recapitulation is made the inevitable climax of the development and is so varied as to take away all feeling of repetition'.[3] Neither do I regard it as a serious blemish that the

[1] In Cobbett's *Cyclopædic Survey of Chamber Music,* Vol. I, p. 390.

[2] *Cours de composition musicale,* Vol. II, part ii, pp. 205-6.

[3] *Loc. cit., supra.*

pianoforte should be found fairly frequently playing in unison with a string part at one or other of its registers, or (more often still) completing, by means of Fauré's usual broken chords, the harmonic scheme sketched out by the strings, as happens for considerable stretches of the *adagio*. There are few pianoforte quintets, or even quartets, in which something of the kind does not occur; and in any case Fauré's practice tended, more and more as his career advanced, towards a presentation of the piano and the strings as complementary rather than rivals to each other. But the finale is by comparison disappointing, and apparently was so to the composer himself. The first performance, given by him with the Ysaÿe Quartet at Brussels in March 1906, was evidently a disappointment to the audience; and Fauré attributed this mainly to a resemblance he had detected between the principal theme of his finale and the *Ode to Joy* melody in Beethoven's choral Symphony.[1] I think he was right; but not in the modest sense that he presumably intended. The movement is, in fact, too much of the family of that deplorable choral finale, and that is precisely what is wrong with it. The theme, embodying (like its model) a kind of rumbustious diatonicism in almost exclusively conjunct movement, belongs to a type even less calculated to draw the best from Fauré than it was from Beethoven; though at first it seems that the situation may be saved by the introduction of a counterpoint to it in the strings:

very much as Beethoven, by means of a similar counterpoint, in his tenor part:

[1] P. Fauré-Fremiet, *op. cit.*, p. 62.

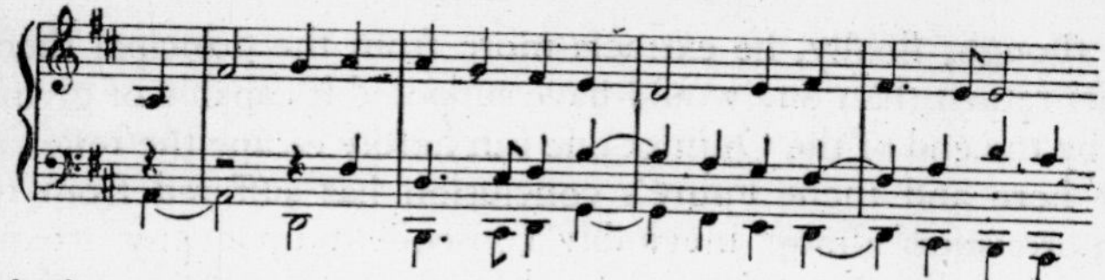

had given promise of a development which in the upshot was never fulfilled. And though Fauré is happier in his middle section, where he first subjects the theme to a series of enharmonic modulations of this kind:

and then introduces a new motive, much more his own in its exploitation of possibilities latent within the diatonic premisses but practically ignored by composers before him:

and though, finally, he extracts more from the principal theme on its return than one would have supposed it capable of giving; yet by the end of the Quintet one can hardly escape the reflexion that here and there Fauré's conclusion has suffered from the clamorousness almost inevitably consequent upon any attempt to emulate Beethoven's celebrated misfire.

What has, however, an important bearing on his own future development is the fact that in this Quintet he had eliminated the scherzo. This seems to have disconcerted his hearers when the work first appeared, and his biographers are inclined to attribute its doubtful reception rather to this frustrated expectation of another movement than to any shortcomings in the finale itself. But it is plain that to Fauré the change of plan was one of deliberate intent, for the rest of his chamber works, with the one exception of the second Quintet, were likewise to consist of three movements only. This modified plan was bound, moreover, to affect his treatment of concluding movements, since in a three-movement form the finale is so comparatively close to the opening *allegro* that to treat it on the same lines, with balanced themes in a binary structure, usually results (in spite of the intervening *andante*) in something like an unresolved duality. Working with four movements it is possible either to conclude with an irresistible burst of high spirits, which was the usual practice of Haydn, or to lead up to a finale which shall fulfil, as it were, the purpose of the whole work by being conceived in more spacious proportions than any of the preceding movements—a scheme frequently adopted by Beethoven, especially in those works which end with a fugue[1] or a set of variations, and also by Franck in his violin Sonata. Fauré himself, in the first Sonata and the two Quartets, had produced finales approximating rather to the Haydn model—though with something less than Haydn's 'irresponsibility'; but in the works of his last period he set himself a task which was not susceptible of a solution along the lines propounded by Beethoven. For the evolution of Beethoven's chamber music was very largely

[1] Into this category falls therefore, pre-eminently, the B flat Quartet Op. 130 in its original form with the *Grosse Fuge* at the end.

towards a modification of traditionally existing forms by elements borrowed from the drama[1]; whereas the parallel with Fauré's later works is rather the choric ode—of the two principles which lie at the base of all art they draw attention rather to unity than to diversity. I cannot therefore agree with M. Koechlin's reproach[2] that his finales attain neither the innocence of Haydn nor Beethoven's unbuttoned expansiveness. I am persuaded that he was not aiming at either. But I do certainly believe that the proposition, imperfectly answered as it seems to me in the finale to the first Quintet, was triumphantly solved in the concluding movements of most of the works which followed it. For what he has done is surely to weld the movement indissolubly to the main body of the work by making it sound—the whole of it, not merely its concluding pages—like a prolonged leave-taking or rounding-off; Stravinsky, it would appear, saw the question in very much the same light when he described the last movement of his *Serenade* for pianoforte as a *Cadenza finale*.

In each of these final movements—to a greater degree even than in the case, already noted, of his opening allegros—Fauré has presented his successive themes not as a contrast or a balance, but rather as the complement or the extension of each other. For example, in the finale of the second violin Sonata the opening theme:

[1] I mean of course the music-drama: what the French in the eighteenth century, and later, called *le théâtre lyrique* with reference, *e.g.*, to Rameau and Gluck.

[2] *Op. cit.*, p. 108. It is curious that one of the only two among Fauré's finales that M. Koechlin can unreservedly admire is the questionable one in the first Quintet. One fears that he may also admire the *Ode to Joy*.

is answered by one which is almost its twin:

the quaver figuration in the piano part, as usual with Fauré remaining constant; in the second violoncello Sonata, having exceptionally dropped the figuration at the approach of his second theme, he guards against any suggestion of a change of mood by marking it *sans ralentir*; while in the first Sonata for the same combination the function of the second theme, as continuing the impetus given by the first, is confirmed not only by similarity of outline but by treating this second theme in canon, so that its rhythmic power is further reinforced:

This canonic presentation—found also in the finale of the second violin Sonata—differs from the familiar example in Franck's Sonata mainly in that Fauré used it not so much for the purpose of developing his theme as for that of confirming the unitary nature of a movement.

This cadenza-like nature of Fauré's finales adds a further significance to his fondness for casting works in a minor key. Of his ten chamber works in extended forms, nine have a minor tonality; and in these nine, either the whole of the last movement or at least its concluding pages will be found to have modulated into the major. This, admittedly, was the frequent practice of both the Viennese-classic and the romantic composers[1]; but not, perhaps, to quite the same purpose. To the romantics the minor was associated with a particular emotional tension from which the major ending came as a relief; to the age of Mozart it was a form to be used only when the character of one's musical ideas specifically called for it[2], the major having become the normal usage. But for the late seventeenth and early eighteenth centuries the minor key was much more normal, because this age had still not lost the memory of the ancient modes, to which our minor—especially in its true form without accidentals, the 'melodic-minor descending' as the textbooks call it—is much closer allied than is our major, for this reason among others that in it the leading-note is an accidental and not a true degree of the scale.[3] Fauré also tended—and more markedly as he grew older—to use the minor scale as a normal means of expression; his achievement as an harmonic explorer may profitably be studied by noticing first of all his desire to avoid the leading-note[4], and the particular value of his slightly unusual education consisted largely in the fact that it also had not forgotten the modes; so that he would bring a work of minor tonality to a major conclusion for the same reason as Purcell or Bach would employ a *tierce de Picardie*—*i.e.*, on the grounds of a musical

[1] Frequent, but not invariable; Mozart's two G minor symphonies, for instance, end in the minor as they began, and so does Brahms's pianoforte Quintet.

[2] I do not think it necessary to assume further that Mozart and his contemporaries regarded the minor as especially apt for subjective expression; I should say that their taste was too good to allow of subjective expression as sufficient ground for any procedure in art. The fact that works in minor keys are with them not only rare but, when they do occur, of a very high average of quality, may surely be explained on the principle that any work of a perfunctory nature would be written in the major as a matter of course.

[3] See p. 53.

[4] 'Ne point conclure au moyen de la sensible', Koechlin, *op. cit.*, p. 160.

logic whose foundations were primarily acoustic, and not in any way sentimental.

The last six of Fauré's chamber works offer a remarkable parallel with Beethoven's last quartets. They represent, like Beethoven's, the highest peak of excellence touched by their composer; they incline, like his, towards a refinement of expression which concedes nothing to the desire for superficial attractions; they met with a certain slowness of acceptance even among many of their composer's own admirers; and at the time of writing them Fauré, like Beethoven, had become deaf. One tends naturally to associate with this last fact, in the one case as in the other, the impression given by these works of having been written down directly from a conception in the brain, without any instrumental corroboration such as Fauré is known to have invoked at the time of writing his first Sonata, when he would work out a passage on Mme. Clerc's piano in the daytime and try it out with Léonard in the evening.[1] They were of course inevitably so written, as is illustrated by the fact that erasures and alterations are less frequent in his later than in his earlier manuscripts[2]; and it may almost be said that they are easier to read than to play. But they are a rare and precious experience for all who have penetrated to their essential meaning. The quintessence of Fauré is in them; power without violence in the opening *allegro* of the second violin Sonata, further exploitations of the ever-widening possibilities of his 'melodico-harmonic'[3] range in the first violoncello Sonata, and in the second an eloquent *andante* which not only repeats but even surpasses the success of the *Élégie*; a Trio as 'tenderly persuasive'[4] as any of his finest songs, a second pianoforte Quintet which was an impressive experience even to those who already knew his greatness, and a string Quartet which, published after his death like a *mémoire d'outre-tombe*, set the seal upon his reputation as a writer of pure music. In these works there are few miscalculations of sonority, but on the other hand instru-

[1] P. Fauré-Fremiet, *op. cit.*, 32-3. [2] *Ibid.*, 82.

[3] As Vincent d'Indy called it: see p. 183.

[4] Florent Schmitt, in Cobbett's *Cyclopædic Survey*, *loc. cit.*

mental 'colour' counts for less than ever, unless it be that of the violoncello in the elegiac movement already described[1]; and there is an even more conspicuous absence of the directions for expression, the complicated phrasing marks and the fussy nuances to which Fauré had in any case never been addicted. The second Quintet is the outstanding evidence of this: in the first movement of this work he was careful, as M. Koechlin observed[2], to mark long stretches *forte sempre* by way of forestalling any lapse into over-'expressiveness'; here as elsewhere in Fauré, and indeed in nearly all the best music, *rubato* is quite out of place, the 'expressive' quality of the works depending on their own 'plastic' features rather than on any inflexions in performance.

Some of their thematic material is adapted from early works which he had discarded; the *andante* of the second violin Sonata, for instance, opens with a theme taken from his Symphony of more than thirty years before, and he used motives from the violin Concerto of an even earlier date in the composition of the string Quartet. The fact that he was able to remodel and transform such youthful material for the purposes of his last phase may perhaps be adduced as proof that these late chamber works are as much the crown of his creative career as they were an augury for the musical future. Certainly he displayed in them all his old skill in turning favourite procedures to advantage; the tritonic melody passage, involving a false relation with the bass, reappears in the first violoncello Sonata:

[1] Even this seems to have been originally a piece for military band, written for the centenary of the death of Napoleon in 1921.

[2] *Op cit.*, p. 115.

the elvish scurrying of the scherzo in Op. 13 is repeated in the corresponding movement of the second Quintet; while in the same movement the relief from this absorbing motion takes the form of an insinuating downward-pointing phrase:

which, like its counterpart in the Trio (codetta of first movement):

shows that Fauré had lost none of his old power in the invention of exquisite falling closes. M. Koechlin's description of the Quintet and the violin Sonata as 'among the first classic works of our own time'[1] may without hesitation be extended to the whole group when one remembers the primary meaning of 'classic'—that is, setting a standard of excellence and serving worthily as a model. Which indeed they did—at a time when

[1] *Op. cit.*, p. 111; M. Koechlin also includes the *first* Quintet under his classification.

the German stock in chamber music had so indubitably exhausted its fertility that each successive work deriving from it was merely achieving a greater degree of stuffiness, so as perhaps to account for the ill-fortunes of chamber music in countries where the German model was still accepted. Neither, to renew for a moment the analogy with Beethoven's last quartets, was Fauré's example quite so completely lost on the next generation in France as was Beethoven's on his immediate successors. One or two of his characteristic procedures even seem in a curious way to have had repercussions farther afield, almost, than we can reasonably suppose his influence to have reached. In the second violin Sonata and the first violoncello Sonata, for example, there is a type of melodic motion, compounded of octaves and single degrees of the scale, which had first announced itself in the 'Fire-motive' of *Prométhée*, and was used again for a theme representating Ulysses in *Pénélope*; it was exploited to the full in the string Quartet and appears to be looking forward to so unlikely a person as our own William Walton. In the Quartet it occurs in all three movements; as a cadential passage towards the end of the first:

as a leading theme in the second:

and in the finale as an accompanying figure which is perhaps the closest approximation to Walton of the three:

Another remarkable musical 'cell' which reached a high stage of evolution in the final period was a scheme of chords following a melody in what the world of the dance-band knows as 'close harmony', and causing the melodic intervals to sound strangely modified because the chord-sequence has followed them in approximately, not exactly, parallel motion. This appears first in the song *Au Cimetière*:

and—something like it having been hinted in the *andante* of the first violoncello Sonata—reaches its fine flower in this soaring passage from the middle movement of the Quartet:

whose monodic strain is so suggestive of a refined operatic tradition that one is tempted to trace similarities with it in those modern Italians who were studying in Paris during Fauré's years on the Conservatoire staff. And there is even, towards the end of the opening *allegro* in the second violoncello Sonata, a kind of stretto, where the cello, having hitherto joined in the ascent towards a peroration, breaks off to reinforce the bass with a series of wide-spaced explosive beats which—but for the fact that the piano continues with its inexorable quaver movement—would seem to have a great deal in common with the device similarly employed to end a movement without rhetorical exaggeration, first by Sibelius in his fifth Symphony[1] and later by Walton and by E. J. Moeran. While finally (and also no doubt as a similar evolution rather than an influence) there are passages in the string Quartet where the parts appear to be moving in order to satisfy the harmonic requirements of a neo-diatonic style in which all the degrees of the scale are of about equal importance:

pointing towards the post-1930 works of Stravinsky and suggesting that in this chamber music of Fauré we may find the key to that 'neo-classicism' towards which others have striven more painfully since his time.

For, by their perfect proportion of structure to content, and by the command of musical language which enables their 'background of calm' to strengthen, if anything, the 'intensity' outlined thereon[2] and invests them with an expressive power owing nothing to any straining of their voice, these works of Fauré's final period are eminently fitted to give a meaning to the term 'neo-classical'. They have as it were reaffirmed without

[1] Which dates from 1915, whereas Fauré's Sonata is of 1922; but even supposing it to have penetrated to Paris, his deafness would presumably have prevented him from hearing it; and in any case I think we are concerned here with a procedure evolved in two places for the same purpose rather than with an actual *influence* in either direction.

[2] See p. 103.

effort an affinity with the pre-Beethovenian era of music, to which certain other composers have found it necessary to stake a claim by the production of somewhat incomplete title-deeds as external evidence; and this while at the same time profiting supremely from the one department of Beethoven's own legacy which, precisely because it was of greatest value for the recovery of artistic tradition after the romantic collapse, had been all but ignored by the musicians of romanticism. It is remarkable how Fauré—apart perhaps from a moment or two in the finale of the Trio—has avoided the error of another chamber work akin to the last quartets of Beethoven: the Quartet by Sibelius, who by an occasional sententious repetition of commonplaces conveys the impression that he has absorbed the vices as well as the inspiration of his model. One feels that it is Fauré's stronger roots in the eighteenth century[1] which have saved him, and enabled him to write the 'first classic works of our own time'.[2] Classic indeed they are, and all the more classic for being essentially *civilized*. Their value in the history of music is all the greater in that they represent an ancient civilization, not an unoriented industrial society nor the disruptive urges of the new barbarism. They reflect no fashion of a time, nor to any great extent the ethos of a race, unless it be the timeless and 'unpolitical' nature (as Thomas Mann would have called it) of the Provençal-Savoyard surroundings in which they were written, and which —so far from being exclusively national—accentuated the identity of the French spirit, as represented in them, with that of civilized humanity. The 'charme antique et durable' of the Annecy landscape, as related by the novelist of the region[3], finds a corresponding note in the unvociferous works produced by Fauré in the retirement of his last years. Their opening movements are vigorous without protestation, their finales joyous without effervescence; and the intervening andantes in particular distil an atmosphere of peaceful intensity, where every vibration is significant without being insistent, by means of a sensitiveness of the 'mind's ear' which renders each turn of the

[1] See pp. 42 and 101. [2] See p. 114.
[3] Henry Bordeaux, *Le Pays natal*, Ch. V.

melodic line more telling on account of the harmonies associated with it:

No music, I think, could better denote that calmness which is so different a thing from dulness, but which had been regularly confused with it by most of the representative romantic figures. Why, asked they (as reported by Alfred de Vigny), was there no middle way between the calmness which wearied them and the passions which made them mad: 'entre la léthargie et les convulsions'?[1] The answer is, of course, that there is, but that no romantic is constituted to discover it; and that the perfect confutation of those who cannot conceive of *le calme* without l'*ennui* is to be found in the unconstrained quietude of this music by Fauré.

[1] Vigny, *Le Mont des oliviers*, l. 110.

CHAPTER VI

THE PIANOFORTE WORKS

THE triumph of romanticism in the earlier part of the nineteenth century had brought about a general lowering of quality in musical composition, seen at its worst perhaps in the opera, and deplorable enough in the solo song, but nowhere more apparent than in writing for the pianoforte. The early history of this instrument did not augur a very promising future for it. From the age of the harpsichord it had inherited a tradition of sonata-writing which the majority of its purveyors preferred more or less to ignore; for though Beethoven tried a few far-reaching experiments with the sonata form (to which no more heed was paid by his immediate successors than to the late quartets), while Clementi and one or two others, such as Hummel, carried on the same form for a few steps in a manner more directly related to the eighteenth-century masters, yet for the most part the sonata was at a discount in the romantic age. It was rejected as not sufficiently 'expressive', or as 'unpoetic', by writers for whom 'poetry' consisted in ignoring constructive or any other logic[1]; and the rapidly growing popularity of the pianoforte was attended instead with a crop of *impromptus* and *fantasias* and *moments musicaux* whose lack of constructive coherence was equalled only by the falsity of the sentiment that was supposed to replace it. The pianoforte 'lyric' was born deformed; and its first years were nursed by composers who imbued it either with mere virtuosity, like Moscheles and Thalberg, or with that mere simpering *espressivo* by which Herz and Hünten (Schumann's 'Philistines') demonstrated all too clearly their own essential affinity with the inaugurators of romanticism.

None of the three notable writers of piano music in the 'thirties and 'forties—Chopin, Schumann and Mendelssohn—

[1] All the more if they were not practising musicians; Mme. de Staël, for example, was satisfied that she had dismissed certain poets beyond appeal by describing their works as 'sonatas in the guise of poems'.

A GROUP WITH ALBENIZ

quite succeeded in living down the *damnosa hæreditas* upon which they had entered. Chopin was always liable upon occasion to succumb to the romantic cult of 'expression'; Schumann never entirely overcame a tendency towards fragmentariness of construction; while Mendelssohn, though his *Songs without Words* are by a very long way the least offensive examples of the type they represent—because they were written by a man with a sense of what was shapely—lacks the savour of really great music because of a certain obstinacy in restricting himself to an harmonic idiom from which the essence had already been fairly thoroughly extracted. All three were immediately influential upon pianoforte writing rather by their 'lyrics' than by their occasional essays in the more completely evolved forms; and of Chopin and Mendelssohn it may be said that their importance for the future of piano music was vitiated to a certain degree by the fact that they helped to transmit the mawkish as well as the delicate element of the *salon* music which, in a superior aspect, they represented. In the case of Schumann, though a similar qualification is true, the valuable element was not delicacy or grace so much as an harmonic savour of precisely the kind that Mendelssohn lacked—Schumann's excursions into suspended and anticipated harmony could at times be quite audacious; but his example counted for less in the formation of Fauré's piano style than that of the other two, and is not as relevant to our purpose here as it was in the matter of the songs, except for a single important work, the Variations. I hope in the course of this chapter to demonstrate that the history of Fauré's pianoforte music provides a parallel to that of his songs in its radical transformation of the *salon* model from which it began, so that by the end of his career the piano lyric had attained as high a degree of evolution, and was capable of carrying as great a significance, as the keyboard sonata of the later eighteenth century. Which is an achievement in which he is approached by none of his contemporaries except possibly Brahms, and by only a very few of his immediate juniors, such as Debussy.

He began with three *Romances sans paroles* (Op. 17) which

E

add nothing to their Mendelssohnian model and therefore appear by comparison to be worth rather less. The earlier works in the forms favoured by Chopin—Impromptus and Nocturnes—tend similarly to reproduce the incidental rather than the individual features of the master who inspired them; but here the situation is complicated, and to a considerable extent saved, by an admixture of just that 'harmonic sensuality' which Ravel applauded in Gounod[1]. A line from the third Nocturne (Op. 33, No. 3) will illustrate this:

And though the second Nocturne takes somewhat after the more languid examples of Chopin in that its progressions are seldom much more than disguised perfect cadences, yet the first (Op. 33, No. 1) in addition to a melodic line pivoted about the dominant of the scale in a manner recalling Duparc (and used again by Fauré at a later date in such works as the song *Arpège*):

[1] See p. 50. I should perhaps add that no derogatory shade whatever is implied by either Ravel or myself in the word 'sensuality', which on the contrary I am anxious to rescue from the discredit of Puritan incomprehension so that it may resume an honourable place alongside

points forward also to one of Fauré's most masterly features in its use of a counter-melody proceeding by suspensions so as to increase the harmonic interest by the very independence of its movement from that of the principal theme:

The fourth Nocturne (Op. 36) is a little too easily satisfied with a 'languid' rather than a 'sensual' opening and with the tonic-and-dominant basis of its second theme, though it has some fine moments where (as in the previously quoted example) the harmonic scheme has its own individuality, so that a drop to the tonic in the melody meets a minor seventh on the supertonic in the accompaniment:

And by the time we arrive at the fifth (Op. 37) we find that Fauré is well on the way to discarding (though not, of course, denying) his models. Apart from a tendency to use a whole musical 'sentence' twice over (found also in one or two other places such as the fourth Nocturne and the second Barcarolle, and corresponding in a way to the habit of symmetrical 'doubling' noticed in the earlier chamber music), this work is already mature both in the organic unity of its structure and in its power of thematic development. The form is one of frequent occurrence in Fauré's piano pieces; a calm first section, recapitulated as a conclusion, and between them a swifter and more disturbed

its counterpart 'spirituality'. The one has as good a right to be exercised as the other

movement[1]; the whole constituting, it will be noted, the exact converse of the ternary form more often found in Schumann and many of the Russians, with whom the 'intermezzo' section is usually the calmer. And an important piece of thematic material not only links the sections together but is developed on its reappearance from the initial *andante*:

to the intermediate *allegro*:

in a way beyond anything in Chopin. Fauré's procedure in development, says one of his critics, is

> neither amplification, as Chopin's sometimes is, nor reduplication, like Schumann's; neither are his pieces, like those of the latter master, made up of a number of fragments in juxtaposition. He thus escapes both mere repetitiveness and mere paraphrase.[2]

In the earlier Barcarolles—which, apart from the first one of all, come farther along the list of his compositions than these Nocturnes—we may observe a more distinctive appearance of Fauré's own individual qualities, partly no doubt because there was a much smaller range of already existing works on which he

[1] M. Jankélévitch noted this form also in the song *Au cimetière* and compared it rather fancifully to a Requiem, the stormy middle section corresponding to the *Dies iræ*. (*Gabriel Fauré et ses mélodies*, p. 100.)

[2] J. Saint-Jean, in *La Nouvelle Revue*, Vol. XIII, p. 263 (1910).

could model himself. Chopin had written only one Barcarolle, and Mendelssohn's scattered examples of *Venetianische Gondellieder* could provide no more than a rhythmic starting-point for a type of composition popular in the early nineteenth century because of its picturesque associations (Rossini had his finger on the public pulse when he inserted one in his opera *Otello*), but hitherto exploited for the sake of those associations without much elaboration of its formal possibilities. Fauré had therefore to draw mainly upon his own presentiments of Venice—a place which, as we know, he did not actually visit until much later[1]—and, correspondingly, upon his own musical invention for all but the barest framework of the Barcarolles. Accordingly, the third contains passages of 'true minor' (with the flat sixth and seventh) alternating with a basic major tonality to produce the true Fauréan evanescence:

the fourth modulates swiftly by means of an insinuating melody which calls for augmented triads to facilitate its progress:

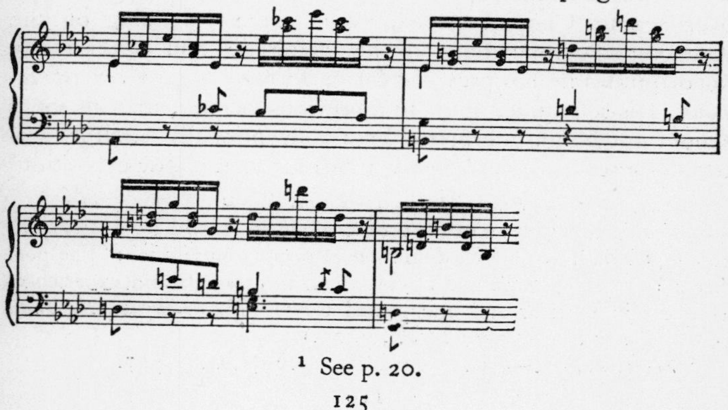

[1] See p. 20.

while in the second there is not only a similar use of the same ambiguous chord for the purpose of sinuous movement, but even an anticipation of the nostalgic suspensions in Debussy's *En bateau*:

Alfred Cortot, though he does not find these works entirely satisfying, supports me nevertheless in regarding them as prophetic of Fauré's future, if only by indicating a departure from previously accepted procedures:

> The development impresses one as perhaps overworked for the type of theme and the evanescent quality of the emotion. . . . There is a kind of inner disharmony about it; but far from deprecating it, we should cherish it with a singular affection, because it was from this uncertain period, this 'awkward age' of M. Fauré's work, that a new beauty was to flower and mature.[1]

Even in those compositions which derive most patently from the Chopin pattern it is possible to discern the capital quality which was ultimately to announce Fauré's original significance over against Chopin: an expressive value depending on the composer's 'combinations of his material'[2] and not on any opportunities he has provided for performers to play *con espressione*. His solicitude, noted in a previous chapter, that his songs should not be misinterpreted by a conventionally 'soulful' performance such as would merely interrupt their plastic exposition[3]

[1] Cortot, *French Piano Music*, 1st series, p. 124.

[2] For this description of the process of composition I have attempted to adapt Mr. T. S. Eliot's definition of poetic composition: 'The poet has a particular medium . . . in which impressions and experiences combine in peculiar and unexpected ways.' (*Tradition and the Individual Talent*, in *Selected Essays*, p. 20.)

[3] See p. 81, and—for this use of the word 'plastic'—p. 7.

has its parallel in the calmness which is said to have characterized his playing of his own piano words, and which Mendelssohn also, we are told, recognized as the essential condition of real musical feeling. 'To have heard Fauré at the piano', wrote M. Koechlin, 'was sufficient to prove that a controlled manner of playing can still allow scope for a great many shades of emotion.'[1] Thus in the third Impromptu (Op. 34) the nature of the harmonic suspensions in the left hand is such that their meaning would be obscured if the player employed the old device of 'pressing' sentimentally upon the right hand appoggiaturas by means of an interference with time-values—lingering on the first beat of a phrase, for example, or separating what is written to be played simultaneously:

Chopin's music is frequently (and most unjustly to Chopin) made intolerable by such pianistic tricks; to apply them to Fauré's music would simply render it unintelligible. Similarly, and in the same piece, the effect of this passage, proceeding through a kind of plagal progression like a pair of wings opening and folding:

[1] Koechlin, *Gabriel Fauré*, p. 190.

would be spoiled by any attempt to emphasize it with *rubato*; even the tenth in the bass (fifth bar) is best *not* spread if the hand can stretch it.

The salutary absence of emphasis and romantic exaggeration in these works of Fauré's first period is proof, if no more, of a negative quality; that he was not a virtuoso composer. His music gives no handle either to virtuosity of technique or to virtuosity of sentiment; of which the latter is the more insidious danger. Difficult of execution it sometimes is; but its 'showing-off' qualities are not such as to compensate a mere *bravura* pianist for the labour involved in learning it. The difficulties are for the most part of the kind that calls, not so much for dexterity of execution, as for comprehension of the musical texture; the music is so constructed that a sense of aural subtleties, rather than any 'muscular memory', is the only guide to the fingers. May not this have been the real ground for the astonishing remark made by Liszt, that Fauré's *Ballade* (Op. 19) was too difficult[1]? Liszt, a virtuoso *in excelsis* both as pianist and as composer, was musically circumscribed (though one hardly supposes that, like Sam Weller, he felt it as a limitation) by a vocabulary and syntax which were really no more than the conventional major-and-minor with a great many chromatic trimmings; so that even a straightforward passage (as it seems to us after sixty years) of this kind:

[1] See p. 15. The *Ballade* is for pianoforte and orchestra, the orchestration (it would seem) being, exceptionally, Fauré's own; but the earlier version for piano alone, differing from the final form only by the absence of one bar of the orchestral part, is still extant, and this is presumably what Liszt saw.

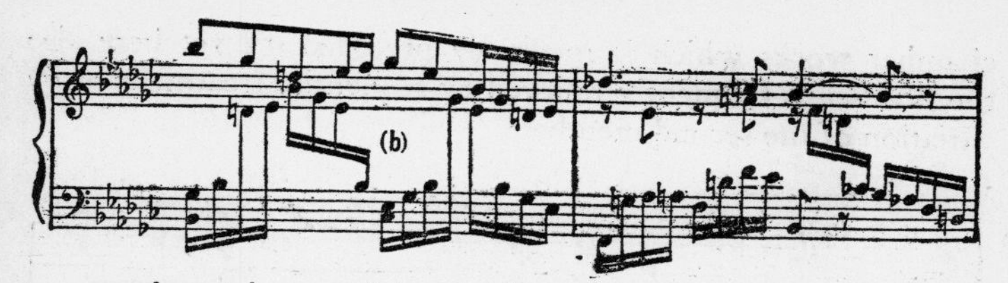

was, perhaps, inaccessible to him because it involves two of Fauré's characteristic devices: the suspension on two notes of the same chord at (a) and the major seventh, not indeed unprepared but somewhat exceptionally resolved, at (b). Liszt's discomfiture over the *Ballade* is rather suggestive of the difficulty found with even the simplest of Fauré's songs—even *Après un rêve*, even *Lydia*—by singers whose experience is confined to German works[1]; and there are others besides Liszt who have found that the Fauré piano music does not meet the desire either for technical display or for emotional exhibitionism, as we may well understand knowing that the composer, writing his pieces with a view to playing them himself, 'had a horror of virtuosity, of *rubato* and of those effects in performance which send shivers down the spine of the audience'.[2] The *Ballade* is much more mature than a good many of the pianoforte works written subsequently to it; at one point indeed in the fourth Nocturne, fifteen opus numbers later, there are a few bars that might almost have been transferred from it:

while, though it is even more given over to the practice of 'parallelism' in double phrases than was the case with the two

[1] See p. 81.
[2] P. Fauré-Fremiet, *Gabriel Fauré*, p. 56.

chamber works which immediately preceded it[1], yet here also the practice is frequently relieved by sequential treatment or by variation of the second member:

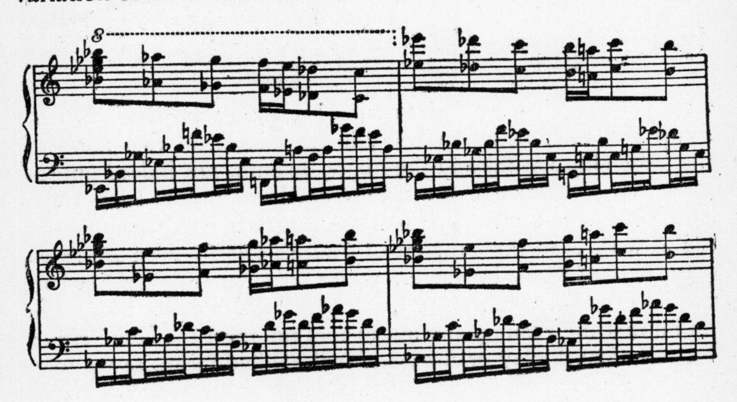

and this at a time when the example of the greater Franck works, which erect this procedure almost into a principle, was not available; for the *Ballade* is as indubitably anterior to the *Variations symphoniques*, which in this and other matters it somewhat resembles, as the violin Sonata by Fauré was to that by Franck. We have it moreover on the authority of J. Saint-Jean[2] that some twenty or thirty years after it was written the *Ballade* was found by critics in France to contain some curiously *pré-debussyste* features; similar, one supposes, to those which I have cited as announcing Debussy in the second Barcarolle.

By the time Fauré entered upon his next phase of pianistic production he had arrived at his full maturity; the second Quartet, the Requiem, the two series of Verlaine songs and some of the theatre music had all been written, and his style in pianoforte composition was beginning not to advertise itself by superficially startling features, but to distinguish itself by reveal-

[1] See p. 95 *ff*.

[2] In *Musica* for February 1909; quoted by Octave Séré, *Musiciens français d'aujourd'hui*, p. 189.

ing unexpectedly fresh aspects of the idiom he had developed out of the *salon* music which was his point of departure. He retained a fondness for the ternary form, previously described, in his pieces; though in the sixth Nocturne it is complicated by an episode within the episode, in the seventh by a reminiscence of the episode in a calmer form by way of conclusion, while in the seventh Barcarolle (Op. 90) the process is no longer one of complication but of levelling-out, the middle section having a different figuration but the same tempo, so that the form, like that of the Bach fugue, becomes not so much ternary as unitary. On rare occasions, as in the fourth Impromptu, he reversed his ordinary process by writing an *andante* episode between two *allegro* sections; and even so it is the *andante* which is the more disturbed in mood, on account of its harmonic tortuousness. His rhythms also tended during this period to a certain complexity; instead of the one beat per triplet (occasionally varied by three beats across a 6-8 bar) of the earlier Barcarolles, the fifth (Op. 66) opens as follows:

and the Nocturnes of the same period are all cast in rather elaborate time-divisions, involving a melody which threads its way with rhythmic ambiguity through an intricate pattern of closely subdivided beats; the most notable example is probably the 18-8 of the seventh Nocturne:

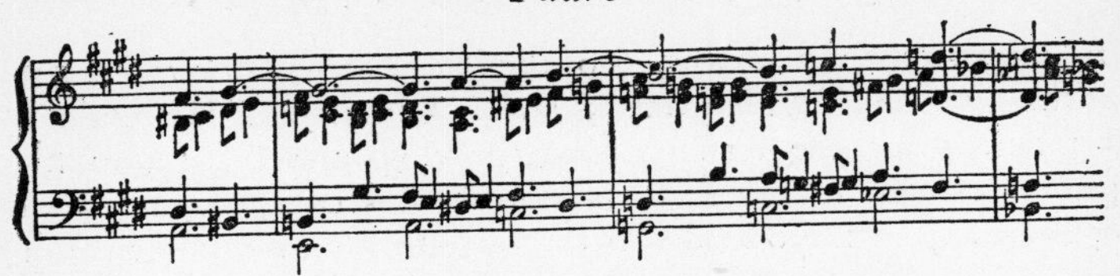

The instrumental melody, over which the *Agnus* of the Requiem is sung, illustrates the same matter.

The quaver or semiquaver figuration of Fauré's piano music fulfils a purpose similar to that of the same feature in the chamber works. Writing for the solo instrument he sometimes employs the device in a special type, consisting of scale-passages running on either side of the melody, as in the seventh Barcarolle:

But for the most part the 'flow' of his music is maintained in its unimpeded tranquillity, its 'background of calm'[1], by a constant use of arpeggio which in some of its more easily recognizable manifestations I have known to be described as a vice. M. Alfred Cortot was aware of the objection:

> He has a habit of writing broken chords to replace simultaneous harmonies, but there is a diversity in the method which constantly renews the interest of an idiom in itself a little monotonous. The linked chords thus written, often shared between the two hands, take on a plastic, astonishing suppleness which seems to arrest the curve of melody emerging from them in mid-air.[2]

Of the abundant examples to my hand, illustrating this element of Fauré's texture, I select this from the sixth Nocturne:

[1] See p. 103.
[2] Cortot, *op. cit.*, p. 113.

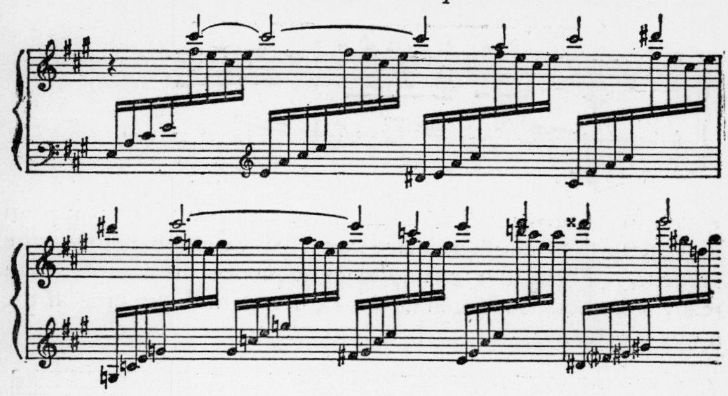

because of its bearing not only on the rhythmic but also on the harmonic implications of M. Cortot's remarks. Besides its contribution to the 'flowing' effect, the arpeggio figuration in Fauré's works assists him to many of his most inventive strokes of suspended harmony or enharmonic change; both of which are found in this passage from the fourth Impromptu, where simultaneous chords would have had a far less insinuating appeal, in addition to sounding more like an intentional innovation:

The importance of suspensions and retardations in Fauré's harmonic schemes is attested also by an extract from the seventh Nocturne:

which in its turn reminds us of the predominant part played in his structures by another device that needs careful handling—the sequence. Those few examples of sequences in Fauré which really sound crabbed, such as this rather painful climbing in the ninth Nocturne:

serve, at any rate, to show by contrast what he could do by means of sequential treatment in a score of other places, of which I need perhaps not adduce any more at this point, since the matter is very well illustrated by any of the three passages quoted on the immediately preceding pages.

The other notable exercise of Fauré's skill in these works is with regard to the *conclusions* of pieces, of their sections or of single musical 'sentences'. The ninth Nocturne, though it does not show him at his best in the sequence, provides a good instance of the flavour he often gives to a piece by ending it with what M. Jankélévitch called 'a final scruple'[1] before coming ultimately to rest on the tonic.

[1] *Op. cit.*, p. 54.

The same critic remarks[1]: 'I can think only of Chopin who brings such delicacy and such coquetry to his concluding passages'; and is perhaps putting his finger unconsciously on what may easily become a fault. For the word *coquetterie*, representing one of the most contemptible of personal qualities, is not very palpably improved by transference to a doubtful behaviour in art. The Revolutionist Siéyès, writing as an experimental philosopher before the Revolution, employed it, with reference to the use of *words* for imaginative purposes, to deprecate 'the coquettish kind of language which draws attention to itself' instead of 'allowing the mental vision to fix itself unobstructedly upon the object'[2]; and may we not adapt this definition—not indeed to what is commonly called 'musical *language*' and which is itself 'the object', the primary material out of which the artistic design is made—but to the manner of announcing a design, which by concentrating attention upon the presentation rather than the thing presented may as surely lead to sentimental deformation of the design as the coquetry of a woman will infallibly turn grace into ugliness? To apply the principle at once to the specifically musical question, is it not true that when a piece of music is presented in such a way that it appears to be saying: 'Observe the unexpectedness of my ending'—or, for that matter, 'Observe the pathetic effect of this passage' or 'Notice the emotion conveyed here'—the result is to destroy our interest in the very thing to which attention is drawn? The same argument which is conclusive against sentimentality in *performance* is also valid against deliberate display *by the composer* of those emotionally affected states which should be the outcome, not the essential matter, of art. I do not think Fauré does this at all frequently; I am quite sure that he triumphantly avoids it, for example, in this brilliant variation (third Impromptu), by means of a skilfully inserted minor seventh, on one of Chopin's best-known formulas for ending a piece:

[1] *Op. cit.*, p. 52.

[2] Quoted by A. Monglond (*Le Préromantisme français*, Vol. II, p. 472), who got it from Sainte-Beuve, *Causeries du Lundi*, Vol. V, p. 198.

I am not so sure of another ending, quoted by M. Jankélévitch from the first Impromptu:

One thinks of Beethoven's trick of an excursion into a remote key just before the end of a movement, which began so deliciously but finally became a mannerism.

It is not, moreover, a reproach to Fauré that his was a conscious as against a 'spontaneous' choice of musical phraseology. A comparatively unimportant department of his output, the four *Valses-Caprices*, may serve at least as proof that his conscious approach to the peculiar idiom, traditionally requisite for such works as these, was precisely what accounted for their superiority over many waltzes by composers who looked at the form, as it were, from inside; and the difference between his music and theirs was, exactly, the distinction of consciousness proper from either self-consciousness or simple spontaneity. Fauré's waltzes conform in many ways to those of Saint-Saëns or even Auguste Durand, which in their turn derive from the type represented by the more superficial of Chopin's *valses brillantes*; in some places the conformity is so close as to involve a melodic phrase coming to rest on the added sixth:

But Fauré has introduced an extra drop of elixir, which if we examine it we shall find to consist in just that *irony* which is simply a form of the 'conscious' or 'contemplative' approach to the subject:

There are waltzes by Russian composers, in particular a celebrated one for two pianos by Arensky (Op. 15, No. 2) whose superiority over the average of ballroom waltzes—depending mainly, I think, on a use of those harmonic suspensions which I have elsewhere called 'nostalgic'[1]—is similarly a matter of a consciously objective treatment of an emotional atmosphere with the ironic judgment of an artist. And there is something like it in one or two other works by Fauré where a melodic line, which in the hands of a less contemplatively detached composer would have resulted in mere archness, takes on a genuinely musical significance; for example this swinging theme from the second Barcarolle:

or, even more appositely, a theme from the second Impromptu (Op. 31):

[1] See p. 126.

which is so excellent an instance of the almost uniquely French ability to write in an initially attractive style without descending to vulgarity, that one thinks at once of similar passages in the work of Fauré's successors, such as this ingratiating tune from the *Pantoum* in Ravel's Trio:

or even of certain pages of Poulenc.

Fauré, then, both in the matter of general shapeliness and on the particular point of rounding off his melodic lines, is conscious of the direction his music takes but does not—except in his weaker works—draw attention to it by coyness of presentation; so that only good can come of our forming a clear notion of the individual directions into which he has guided it. Foremost among these I would place the fact that with him there is no longer any great conclusiveness attaching to the perfect cadence. As we have seen[1], this was so exhausted an element of musical phraseology that Fauré frequently preferred to avoid it altogether; and when he does use it, it is with no emphasis or sense of finality. He never keeps us waiting for the resolution of the dominant to the tonic chord; in fact rather the reverse, for he will lead up to the cadence by such uncommon steps that the latter of its harmonies is sounding almost before we realize that we have arrived at the former:

[1] In Chapter III; and also in connexion with the chamber music, see pp. 95 and 111.

Alternatively, having reached what used to be called 'a full close', he is frequently not satisfied until he has established the tonic harmony by means of some subsequent and different steps. A fairly early example of this is provided by the fifth Nocturne.

another by the concluding bars of the sixth, while as a further illustration from Fauré's latest period I may quote from No. 2 of the Preludes Op. 103, where the resolution of the leading-note is scarcely more than touched upon, and, even so, followed up by two more cadential progressions before the piece is brought to a close:

His invention of ways of leaving and returning to his original tonality is almost inexhaustible; and so great is his skill in recovering the tonic that he does not hesitate to leave it very early in a piece. The eighth Nocturne (No. 8 of a miscellaneous album of *Pièces brèves*, collected as Op. 84 but written at various dates) begins in D flat[1] but has already reached a suggestion of a kind of Phrygian mode on C in its second bar:

And from No. 1 of the same *Pièces brèves* I transcribe a passage typical of Fauré's 'easy recovery'[2], which may serve as a specimen to represent a great many others:

This is one of his outstanding abilities as against, for example,

[1] Fauré was almost unique in being able to make something of this favourite key of his. Has any other composer done so much to enable the last three flat keys to live down their pervading atmosphere of *Soupirs* and *Liebesträume?*

[2] There is also, in No. 3 of the *Dolly* suite for pianoforte duet, a charming effect of recovered tonality where, just before leaving the alien key, Fauré introduces a quotation from the finale of his first violin Sonata.

Berlioz, whose music frequently sounds uneasy through being at the same time very anxious to return to the tonic harmony and very awkward in its method of doing so. The feature was singled out for notice by J. Saint-Jean in his previously quoted article on the piano music: 'Often, having reached the most distant key possible, he makes a supple *volte-face* and returns to the principal key by the shortest, most unexpected and most picturesque road'[1], and was described excellently by M. Koechlin as 'the unfailing grace of a cat falling on its feet'[2], which is the best expression of a comparison repeated by a great many of Fauré's critics. Émile Vuillermoz was one of the earliest: 'His indolent grace and cat-like flexibility conceal a great exactitude and lucidity of purpose.'[3] And M. Jankélévitch appears to have combined these two judgments into one: 'However Fauré's music may tremble in its balance, it always falls on its feet, with the flexibility and precision of a cat.'[4] It is also a point in common among his various critics that they are all given to comparing the impressions made by his music with iridescent or opalescent reflections such as those from the uncertain surface of *moiré* silk. But however this echoing of each other may lose currency for their phrases, I have sometimes thought that Fauré's music might be very exactly qualified by comparing it to the nature of that exquisite animal, the cat[5]. Strength without brutality; muscles which achieve grace all the more perfectly because they do not have to strain after it—these are essentially feline traits; and on the less tangible side a demand for understanding before it will yield you its companionship, and a distinction of character which prevents it from being degraded to the function either of a mere toy or of a mere stimulant.

Fauré's most ambitiously proportioned work for pianoforte

[1] *La Nouvelle Revue*, Vol. XIII, p. 258 (1910).
[2] *Op. cit.*, p. 105.
[3] *La Revue musicale*, October 1922. [4] *Op. cit.*, pp. 59-60.
[5] And even that the aptness of this comparison might give a clue to the slow welcome afforded to Fauré in a country where the national character expresses itself in a love of dogs and horses.

solo is a Theme and Variations (Op. 73) to which English audiences have taken more kindly than to the Nocturnes and Barcarolles for the very reason, perhaps, that it is nearer allied to the musical models of their previous preference and rather less characteristic of its composer's own individuality. It bears a striking resemblance—partly through being written in C sharp minor—to the *Études symphoniques* of Schumann; and though one may observe some of the more properly Fauréan qualities by closer examination, yet the likeness does not on that account disappear. Fauré's theme, like Schumann's, is binary, each of its sections coming to rest on the tonic chord, and the variations, also like Schumann's, retain this pattern throughout; with the result that the work contains a higher proportion of full closes than any other by its composer. He has, moreover, accepted the variation form with as little modification as he brought to the sonata form in his earlier chamber works[1]; there is no attempt at radical transformation of structure such as we find, for instance, in the variations of B. J. Dale's two Sonatas. On the other hand the restricted outline seems to have allowed Fauré what scope he wanted for a variety of mood-changes; and his plainest departure from Schumann, or for that matter from the type of romantic variations in general, such as Glazunov's, is that he has chosen to end the series on a peaceful note rather than with a flourish. Otherwise the comparison may be pursued almost step by step; in one variation the melody of the theme is made to serve as a bass, in another the resemblance is contradicted only by Fauré's favourite modulation to a scale of flattened degrees:

[1] See p. 95.

and the closest parallel of all with Schumann is that of the tenth variation, a scherzo in 3-8 time with its melody in the tenor register, where the likeness to Schumann's ninth *Étude* extends even to the scamper down the keyboard near the end. The finest and most individual of the variations is probably the ninth, with its 'dying fall' centring upon a curiously consolatory chord of the thirteenth at (a):

which bears, for Mr. Edwin Evans also, 'the stamp of Fauré's personality' and which M. Alfred Cortot described as 'sinking down like a star in the evening'.

The *Pièces brèves* had been a sublimation of those *morceaux de salon* among which Fauré had grown up; the *Préludes* (Op. 103) on the other hand look forward to a type of composition which we associate with the generation of his pupils and juniors rather than his own. They bear much the same relation to the rest of his work that Chopin's Preludes do to his, which is to say that they contain some of his purest and strongest music. They are unitary in form and single in mood; and for the most part they are evolved from musical 'cells' rather than extended themes, a feature which they share with the finest of the Preludes by Rakhmaninov; consider this building-up of interest from No. 1, in that key of D flat without at least one example of which no Fauré collection would be complete:

M. Cortot writes of their 'grave serenity'; and of No. 6, in E flat minor (the original three Preludes of 1910 were increased to nine the next year), Mr. Aaron Copland does not hesitate to say that it 'can be placed side by side with the most wonderful of the Preludes of the *Well-tempered Clavichord*'.[1] No. 5, in D minor, which M. Koechlin[2] singled out as unusual in Fauré's music for the forceful, even angry mood it suggests, is notable also for a richness of figuration having a particularly Rakhmaninovian flavour and clarified towards the end into a liturgical-sounding passage recalling the *Libera* of the *Requiem*; while in No. 2 (C sharp minor) the harmony is such that at one or two points it suggests the whole-tone scale.

Approximations to that hotly-discussed piece of musical syntax occur for more than one reason in the piano music written by Fauré in his early sixties. One is his fondness for chords, such as the augmented triad, which may occur in the course of a whole-tone scheme; this provides an example as early as the seventh Nocturne, written in 1898:

[1] *The Musical Quarterly* (New York), October 1924.
[2] *Op. cit.*, p. 92.

Another is his addiction to sequential passages at distances of one tone, observable in the eighth Barcarolle (Op. 96):

where not only the sequence but the *appoggiature* contribute to the effect. The culmination of this tendency is in the fifth Impromptu (Op. 102), where the sequences hint at the scale while the accompanying passage-work traverses it entire. J. Saint-Jean[1] calls this 'a curious effort to incorporate the whole-tone scale into the traditional system'; but it appears to me rather as the logical outcome of the freedom with which Fauré had discovered fresh significances in that system. However that may be, he did not exploit the discovery at all systematically; the only other noteworthy use of it is in his second work for pianoforte with orchestra, the *Fantaisie* Op. 111.

This work, in which the *vaporeux* quality noticed by some critics in the *Ballade* has been replaced by an astringency almost announcing Roussel, exemplifies several of the procedures typical of Fauré's latest manner. The form is his familiar ternary one, and many of the old devices of figuration recur, such as the scale-passages crossing and recrossing the melodic line, and the indispensable broken chords; these, however, are of a thinner texture and modified by suspensions and passing-notes, as in the pianoforte writing of the late chamber works.

[1] *Loc. cit., supra*, p. 268.

The augmented triad as a modulatory instrument is here also, as are the *appoggiature* at one tone's distance, employed so as frequently to involve the tritone. These account for the characteristic melodic curve of the principal subject, whose latter end depends moreover on a sequence of two of them one tone apart, analogically to the foregoing extract from the eighth Barcarolle:

In the recapitulatory section there are moments where this answering of the subject one tone lower has been absorbed into the theme itself:

while in the first section there had been, as it were half-way towards this, a stretch of canonic imitation between the solo instrument and the orchestra:

whose penultimate tritonic group is taken up in a kind of final *stretto* to form the basis of a genuine whole-tone-scale passage:

And between the two sections here analysed is an episode in rapid triple time, beginning with a fierce dotted rhythm which eventually resolves into a resistless quaver movement whose only rival in Fauré's music is that of the second Quintet written not long after.

The *Fantaisie*—seldom played though it is, even in France—stands to the piano music of Fauré's old age in much the same relation as the *Ballade* to that of his youth; and its spareness of texture, in comparison with the earlier work, is a feature it shares with many other of his productions in those last years which were so very far from being a decline. The concluding numbers in his series of Barcarolles breathe, in their placid though alert *allegretto* movement, an atmosphere of tranquillity without fatigue, in accordance with the mind of a composer whose capacity to open up fresh vistas of his art, without appearing merely experimental, was confirmed by the evolution of his previous career. In a style whose relation to the piano writing of a dozen years earlier recalls that of the *Chanson d'Ève* to the Samain songs, the ninth Barcarolle—a purely unitary movement evolved from a single theme—develops its original phrase within the first five degrees of the minor scale into quietly expanding passages of this kind:

while the tenth, perhaps the loveliest of them all, irrefutably justifies one of Fauré's favourite procedures in that it twice returns to its main theme by means of long sequences, the one of six limbs, the other of seven, but both of them saved from monotony by the originality of their harmonic succession; the whole sinking to rest by means of this ineffably peaceful cadence:

The last of all the Barcarolles (No. 13, in C major, the treatment of its tonality somehow according perfectly with the idea of an old man saluting a new dawn) has this in common with the string Quartet[1] that it suggests in places the neo-diatonic idiom of the most recent works of Stravinsky:

which occasionally, one must admit, involves a certain melodic inconclusiveness comparable to that which I have attributed to Berlioz[2], though deriving no doubt from the exactly opposite cause. There is moreover in the eleventh Barcarolle one apparent miscalculation which may perhaps be legitimately laid to the

[1] See p. 117. [2] See p. 141.

charge of Fauré's deafness; the logic of the following bars would seem to depend upon a differentiation of *timbre* between the parts, and a contrast of *sostenuto* with semiquaver sonorities, impracticable at such a high register of the keyboard:

Of more profitable commerce to the pianist is the device of writing an *appoggiatura* (occurring either in a plain chord or as part of a scale passage) to be struck simultaneously with another note of the harmony standing at only a tone's or a semitone's remove from it. This practice, observable at least as early as No. 4 of the *Pièces brèves*[1], is carried on through the eighth Barcarolle:

and may also be detected in the line already quoted from the thirteenth.

It is used, in a particularly insistent form, to determine the prevailing mood of the twelfth Nocturne:

[1] Known as *Adagietto*; but the fanciful titles of the *Pièces brèves* were, like so many others of their kind, a later addition by the publisher.

which, with its companions of the final period, contrasts sharply with the vesperal contentment of the Barcarolles. The nocturne form had come increasingly, in the course of Fauré's career, to signify for him something of the gloom of night as well as its quietude; and these last Nocturnes are the fulfilment of that tendency—M. Koechlin[1] goes so far as to describe their mood as one of despair. One of them, the eleventh, is explicitly a funeral elegy—on the young wife of Pierre Lalo—and performs this function by means of an idiom which is the culmination of Fauré's enharmonic style:

while the tortured harmony of the twelfth would seem to render it appropriate to a very similar purpose:

They are the only department of his work in which one may, with considerable reason, see a revolt against age and approaching dissolution; and I know of no musical parallel to them in this respect unless it be the strident passage at the climax of Holst's *Saturn*.

[1] *Op. cit.*, pp. 102 and 192.

The analogy may perhaps be carried a little farther. *Saturn* comes to a restful conclusion; and the thirteenth Nocturne (Op. 119), though it also rises to a cry of Promethean lamentation—not as terrible as that of the twelfth, for its ambiguous tonality conveys rather a questioning than a despairing mood:

—subsides at the end into an eloquent falling close:

which is indeed the epilogue to a tragedy, but which has also the tragic virtue of conveying a sense of completeness rather than frustration. *Consummatum est*, it seems to say; and with this word it completes a series of works which have some title to be regarded as the consummation of the pianoforte lyric.

CHAPTER VII

WORKS FOR LARGER FORCES

It is not without justification that Fauré has been regarded, both in and outside his own country, as primarily a writer in the smaller forms. I do not wish to enlarge here on the question whether music for chamber ensemble should properly be described as belonging to the 'smaller forms' in any respect but that of the number of performers required—even so, it was not until Fauré's very last years that his supremacy in this type of composition became as evident as it had been for some time in the songs—and in any case such a valuation need not cause either a feeling of surprise or a sense of injustice when applied to a composer who had destroyed his solitary attempt at a Symphony; refused to publish, and perhaps never completed, the violin Concerto with which he had followed up the success of his first Sonata; and put an obvious gap between himself and the generality of French composers by resolutely declining for a long time to write for the operatic stage. The result was that when *Prométhée* appeared it was immediately declared in many quarters to be outside his province, which rendered more difficult than it might otherwise have been the task of assessing it on its own merits. The usually enthusiastic Émile Vuillermoz wrote regretfully that Fauré had 'put more of his essential self into *Soir* than into the whole of the *Prométhée* music'[1]; and one cannot say categorically that this judgment was due to a preconceived notion of the 'essential self'. What it does indicate is an excessive regard for recognizably subjective qualities in art; in contradistinction to which, if any valuable criticism of *Prométhée* is to be reached, one may hope to bear in mind rather its fitness for its individual purpose as well as those standards of musical invention and significant form which are the same for all music, whatever its framework.

[1] *La Revue illustrée*, 1st July 1905; quoted by Séré, *Musiciens français d'aujourd'hui*, p. 190, and by Koechlin, *Gabriel Fauré*, p. 130, n.

Fauré's own apprehension that his work would sound like an imitation of Wagner is all the more understandable when we remember that Wagner's achievement had been along the very lines that this work followed: in his mythological music-drama (at its best; we are able nowadays to discriminate about him more than they generally did in 1900) music, for the first time since the trombones in *Don Giovanni*, had been solemn, in the better sense of the word—a sense more nearly approaching, perhaps, to Wagner's own *feierlich* if we substitute the word 'hieratic'—without becoming pompous or bombastic. What wonder, therefore, that one seeking to steer the same course and avoid the same dangers should employ something resembling Wagnerian methods?—*e.g.*, this use of what was conventionally called the 'leading seventh', though for Wagner already its fundamental was more often treated otherwise than as a leading-note:

I think, however, that the Ocean Nymphs' chorus, reminiscent as it is of nothing so much as of Fauré's own delicately flowing songs—such, for instance, as that very *Soir* in comparison with which Vuillermoz dismissed it—may fairly be given credit for an originality over against the Rhinemaidens and also for an appropriateness to the subject it illustrates:

and from the rest of the score I would select for special notice the motive standing for the Theft of the Fire:

because of its wide melodic swing, belonging more or less to the family of the first subject in the A major Sonata, and contrasting strongly with the Nymphs' chorus and other passages of Fauré in which a movement of rather small intervals is modified in its direction by the harmony attending it[1]; and the following characteristic stride, as of Prometheus himself among the rocks:

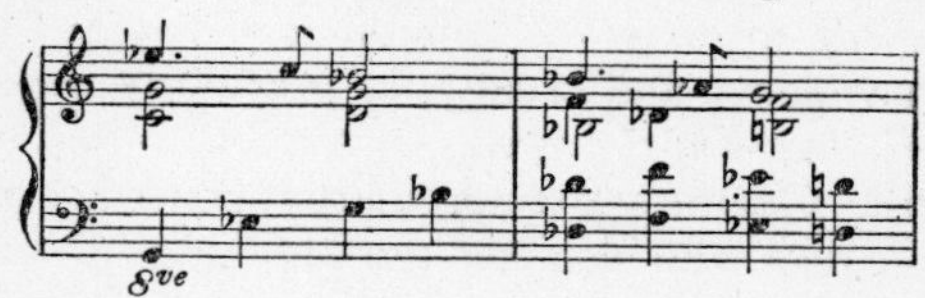

on account of the opportunity it provides to open what must after all be the central question in any discussion of this music: does it match the elemental strength of its story? I have never seen a performance of *Prométhée*; but I am persuaded that the Aeschylean legend will at least suffer no detriment from music of the type I have just quoted, one of whose virtues is that, unlike the lady in *Hamlet*, it does not protest too much. In so far as Fauré's writing for this purpose is successful at all, its success will depend on its attainment of force without violence; and there is a great deal to be said for such a treatment of even the most primitive myth. We should not wish him to envisage the subject as though he were himself a barbarian, any more than the Greek tragedians did; and this will be found to be a particular case of the general principle, that it is a positive disadvantage for an artist to identify himself entirely with the dispositions represented by the subject-matter of his art. From first to last, the legend of Prometheus has been most forcefully illustrated by civilized artists *commenting* on its barbarism; which is further evidence in support of what was described in the previous

[1] See p. 116.

chapter as 'the contemplative approach'. Sometimes, in their anxiety to prove that Fauré was of greater account than a charming miniaturist, his friends attempt to claim for him quite irrelevant qualities. We may agree with M. Koechlin that the D minor Prelude (Op. 103, No. 5) is 'the image of anger'[1], but it would be no artistic credit to Fauré to suppose that he felt angry when he wrote it; for to have *experienced* an emotional state is not as relevant to art as to have *comprehended* it. Neither would the music he provided for Prometheus or for Kratos and Bia be improved by embodying in its own nature the violent daring of the one or the violent cruelty of the others. It is by thus preserving in his work something of the spectator's viewpoint upon violence and cruelty, as previously upon tenderness and languor, that Fauré has shown himself to be a civilized and classic artist. Goethe's extraordinarily penetrating distinction of the classic poet who 'depicted terrible things' from the romantic poet of his own day, who 'depicted things in a terrible manner'[2], applies exactly to Fauré. And it was because hitherto, in that province of music with which he was familiarly associated, he had not committed the artistic error of dealing with soft things softly, that there was at any rate nothing fundamentally unsuited in his style to the proposition 'Prométhée est la force' when he turned his attention to it; any more than the preoccupation of Delius with idylls and summer gardens was in itself a bar to the appropriateness of his music for the Nietzschean precept: 'Wax ye hard!' Much more indeed was it to be feared that Fauré in his writing for these new conditions might lose the subtle flavour of his previous work. That he had, fortunately, not lost it, was the opinion of Pierre Lalo:

> Might not his charm evaporate in the immense space of an open-air theatre? It has not happened so . . . M. Fauré has refused to modify his habitual manner by making it coarser or more ponderous, and yet he has managed to give it the external simplicity that it needed in order to be

[1] Koechlin, *op. cit.*, p. 92. See also p. 144.

[2] Quoted by H. Trevelyan, *Goethe and the Greeks*, p. 163.

> apprehended by a large public. . . . The most cogent examples of this are, certainly, the funeral procession of Pandora[1] and the Ocean Nymphs' chorus. In these two scenes there is no striving after big effects, neither are they without harmonic subtlety; and in both there is a purity of melodic line which has not been spoiled by the distance or the size of the theatre.[2]

And from the fact that Lalo was usually well disposed towards Fauré's music, as also from the fact that he has here singled out for special praise the quieter episodes of *Prométhée*, I leave my readers to draw what conclusions they think fit.

Whatever may have been Fauré's qualifications for measuring himself with this large-scale subject, his previous contacts with dramatic music had demanded a capacity of just the opposite kind: a capacity, that is, to write in a manner that should be slight without triviality. Incidental music for a play has always a Scylla and a Charybdis besetting it; it must not be so lacking in substance as to be devoid of interest, and it may not attract the exclusive interest to itself that is permissible in opera—neither is it possible as a rule to assume anything like the vocal abilities of operatic performers when the score contains voice-parts, as Grieg for example was plainly aware in his music for *Peer Gynt* and as even Delius was obliged to admit to the extent of slightly modifying the inaccessibility of his vocal writing in *Hassan.* Fauré's music for *Caligula* (Op. 52) includes two choruses for a kind of ballet interlude, sung by figures representing the Hours; they are wisely confined to a unison line, but the Day Hours are allotted a martial entry whose simplicity is yet not such as to leave any doubt of its authorship:

[1] After her rejection by Prometheus in the first act, Pandora dies; and it is evidently a constructive fault that the reasons for bringing her to life again in the later part of the drama are not made sufficiently clear.

[2] *Le Temps*, 5th October 1900.

while the lulling strain given to the Night Hours is even more recognizably related to the unprepared or exceptionally resolved sevenths of Fauré's most voluptuous songs:

Shylock is still better; in Haraucourt's play rather more is made than in the Shakespearean original of the 'masques and revels' which gave Lorenzo the chance to steal away Jessica, so that in addition to a care-free carnival song whose burden is 'Les baisers défendus, c'est Dieu qui les ordonne', we have a delightful *entr'acte* in which a pianissimo trumpet figure, sounding like a signal to revelry, alternates with a piquant melody whose fluctuating tonality consorts perfectly with the evasive *fête-galante* atmosphere

afterwards evoked in *Mandoline*; while perhaps the crown of the *Shylock* music is a little Nocturne for strings alone, a kind of untroubled and more moonlit version of the crepuscular *Soir*, whose opening phrase it prefigures in the clearer key of D as against D flat major:

These *Shylock* pieces make an excellent suite for concert purposes; and those that Fauré wrote nearly ten years later for *Pelléas et Mélisande* make, if anything, a better, for though the *Sicilienne* was originally an independent composition, it is as though made for its position between the *Fileuse* (the taste for instrumental 'spinning songs' had still not died out in 1898) and the *Adagio* which accompanies the death-scene of Mélisande in the last act. The former of these two movements has a melody of such Fauréan individuality, in its rapid departure from and recovery of the tonic, that it reduces the wheel-humming effect to a properly secondary importance; and in the latter of them a sense of unity is further encouraged by thematic transference, in that the end of one section in the *Fileuse*

and the opening phrase of its middle episode[1]

are combined in the reverse order at the climax of the *Adagio*:

this last movement being moreover introduced and closed by a

[1] For the *Fileuse* I quote from M. Cortot's pianoforte transcription.

liturgical-sounding theme which Fauré had not forgotten at the time of writing the *Chanson d'Ève*[1]:

Slightly earlier than any of this theatre music—written indeed a year before the *Requiem*, though published after it as Op. 50—is a *Pavane* for small orchestra with optional choir, described by the composer himself as 'carefully wrought, but not otherwise important'[2], yet nevertheless significant by the same right as some of the Verlaine songs because it is a further proof of Fauré's ability, shared with so many French artists of his time, to recreate the past (especially the age of the Rococo) without lapsing into an affectedly 'period' manner of expression[3]. The words are a Versailles-pastoral conversation of no great poetic value, and the *Pavane* is usually played without them; but in either form it conveys a peculiarly poignant nostalgia by its alternation of sharp with flat sixths and sevenths and by cadential writing of this kind:

which in its sinuous, unimpeded movement and its absence of sentimental lingering so well illustrates a line of the text: 'La cadence est moins lente, et la chute plus sûre.'

Not the least fascinating part of this little piece is the orchestration, with its sensitive differentiation of wood-wind *timbres*;

[1] See p. 83.

[2] In a letter to Mme. Baugnies, quoted by P. Fauré-Frémiet, *Gabriel Fauré*, p. 45.

[3] See p. 68.

but is it Fauré's own? The scoring of a great many of his works is known to have been entrusted to colleagues or pupils; *Pelléas et Mélisande* to Charles Koechlin, *Prométhée* to the bandmaster Eustace and *Pénélope*—to whom? Philippe Fauré-Fremiet[1] writes as though his father had, at least in part, orchestrated the opera himself; M. Koechlin[2] suspected (for he gives no evidence) the collaboration of a friend, perhaps d'Indy or Dukas. The six piano-duet pieces called *Dolly*[3] were scored, for the purpose of a ballet, by Henri Rabaud, Fauré's successor in the Conservatoire directorship; and when René Fauchois, the poet of *Pénélope*, put together a heterogeneous entertainment of a Watteau-Verlainian cast for the Opéra-Comique, entitled *Masques et bergamasques*[4], Fauré's music for the production —besides a newly written Overture and three other numbers (Op. 112)—included the *Pavane* and the obviously appropriate song *Clair de lune*, whose orchestrated version is apparently from his own hand but does not improve upon the piano part. The scoring of a more or less negligible choral cantata of his first period, *La Naissance de Vénus* (Op. 29), is quite without distinction, the strings and the wind frequently doubling each other; and we have already seen that Fauré elected to suppress his larger orchestral works, except a single movement from a Suite (Op. 20) which he reissued as *Allegro symphonique* (Op. 68), but which adds nothing to his reputation. Orchestral conditions in France, for the greater part of his life, were not such as to encourage the composer; one of the obstacles which the Société Nationale was founded to overcome was the unwillingness of orchestral concert-givers to venture beyond established 'classics', and even so the Society was able to afford the expense of only a very few symphony concerts per year. In Fauré's youth, moreover, and indeed considerably later, French musical education tended to neglect the orchestra except for a strictly limited theatrical function, and even at the École Niedermeyer, where

[1] *Op. cit.*, p. 77. [2] *Op. cit.*, p. 174.

[3] Written for, and dedicated to, the small daughter of that same Emma Bardac who was afterwards the second wife of Debussy.

[4] A title derived from a line of Verlaine's poem *Clair de lune*.

this operatic bias was in disfavour, there was a sufficiently strong bias in the contrary direction of church and organ music to reduce symphonic studies to a position of relative unimportance, though Fauré in writing his own account of the school did mention orchestration among the subjects taught. Neither was he one of those who, like Berlioz or Bax, take to the orchestra as the proverbial duck to water; chamber music and songs with piano remained his first loves throughout. We have seen in connexion with his chamber works[1] that instrumental *timbre* was not an object of his closest interest; and the most one can say, to remind orchestral devotees of his value even in this province, is that his music often answers surprisingly well to the orchestral care taken of it by his coadjutors; consider this piece of scoring for the harp in the Prelude to *Pelléas*:

A whole essay might be written to contrast the function of the harp for French composers with its use by Wagner, for example, as ancillary to a surge of symphonic sound; but the place for it is doubtless not in a book on Fauré. What is worthy of note before leaving the subject is his use of the organ in the *Requiem*, where it serves partly to replace the wood-wind but especially as a groundwork to the score in a manner recalling the *continuo* parts of the eighteenth century. In this and in certain allied matters the orchestration of the *Requiem* has an affinity with methods commonly employed in the age of Bach and Handel; the brass is used for a few well-defined entries and remains silent for the rest of the time, much as Bach would write for a horn, or for two *oboi d'amore*, in a single movement only of an extended work.

[1] See p. 101.

The instruments, moreover, support the voices in a way suggest-ing the practice of a century and a half before Fauré's day—and due no doubt simply to the experience of a choirmaster; i is not only harmonic complexity, I think, which led Delius (tc take the most notable among many who had not been trainer of choirs) to write vocal and instrumental parts which resolutely refuse to trespass on each other's territory. The choir of th *Requiem* finds its task technically eased by the orchestra, an most of all by the organ; so that from the example of this ai to the performer—though no music would suffer more tha Fauré's from artistic incomprehension—we may understan also how a chorus consisting mainly of amateurs was able t acquit itself well of the anything but commonplace materia with which it was confronted in *Prométhée.*

Pénélope suffers from its date. It was written between 1907 and 1913—at a time when opera, more than at any other perio of its history, had lost its orientation. The dazzling prestige o Wagner's personal success was found impossible to square wit the equally undoubted fact that neither Wagnerism, no *verismo*, nor any other attempt to come to terms with th 'realistic' theatre can ever furnish a satisfactory foundation fo an operatic style. Debussy's principle, that there was no mor reason for the music—especially the orchestra—to reflect th passions of the drama than there was for the scenery to be con-vulsed when a character came upon the stage, was mostly o negative value, had not been followed out consistently by Debuss himself and will perhaps be more immediately fruitful when if ever, opera enters upon the completely fresh phase for whic it is waiting. Fauré, certainly, was not able in *Pénélope* to neglec the realistic tradition. His text obliged him to open with ye another of those 'spinning choruses' so dear to the romanti opera, since the inevitable explanatory scene at the beginning i given to Penelope's handmaidens who deliver their comment during a session with their spinning-wheels; and he wrote i comic exasperation that it was surprising 'how hard one had t work on a description of people who were scarcely working a all'.[1] He constructed his music for this scene so that, 'according as the words refer to one or another of the characters, the music should indicate to *whom* they refer'; which, with a great deal else in *Pénélope*, points to an extensive use of the *Leitmotiv* system. Here, as with *Prométhée*, Fauré was very well aware of the dangers attending a too close dependence on Wagnerian methods; the trouble was that he had not—as indeed who had at the outset of this century?—a very clear notion as to which part of Wagner's example was more worth following. In a purely musical sense he owes very little to Wagner, for the *Leitmotive* which might appear to be the most obvious borrowing belong, after all, to a line of evolution to which Wagner gave a name but of which he was not strictly speaking the inventor. Here are a few of them; first, the theme associated with Ulysses:

and strongly reminiscent of the Fire-motive in *Prométhée*; then a phrase, of mainly harmonic reference, representing the desolation of Penelope:

and perhaps the nearest to Wagner of the whole work; finally the motive of Penelope's longing for the return of Ulysses, which appears first towards the end of Act I:

[1] This and the following extract from Fauré's own commentary on *Pénélope* are taken from a number of his letters to his wife, quoted by P. Fauré-Fremiet, *op. cit.*, pp. 73-8.

and is transformed at the close of the opera into this triumphant pæan of victory:

The general texture of the music is also far from Wagnerian; a good deal of the recitative tends to pivot on single notes in a manner which might suggest Debussy were it not that the orchestral part is less attenuated:

and the pace of the words, as with nearly all French opera, is much more rapid.

But where Fauré betrays himself as living (operatically speaking) in the still not disillusioned world of Wagnerian discipleship is in his unquestioning acceptance of Wagner's principle of continuity. We can see better after another thirty years that Wagner's own successes were scored rather in spite of this principle than because of it; even, paradoxically enough, that it was really appropriate only to such an art as Debussy's which made little or no pretension to symphonic construction, but corresponded rather to those Chinese pictures of which only a certain length is intended to be unrolled and contemplated at a time; and that as soon as it is applied as an obligatory condition of dramatic music it is liable to result in mere formlessness. But of all this Fauré was, necessarily, not so conscious. He complained of the 'tagged' effect of a rhymed text; he identified thematic significances with dramatically relevant motivation to such an extent as to exclude much of what might otherwise have been musical outline; and while engaged on writing *Pénélope* he wrote a review of Rimsky-Korsakov's *Snow-Maiden* in which, blaming the piece for its lack of continuity, he came nearer than anywhere else I have seen to taking an uncritical point of view:

> *Snegurotchka* is conceived in accordance with the old operatic formula. In it the music is not developed continuously; it is interrupted and divided into sections, joined together by recitatives; each scene, and even each fragment of a scene, could be separated from the work to form a complete whole.[1]

Which is rather as though one should complain of Fauré's own sonatas because they do not, like those of Delius, conform to the telescopic one-movement type introduced by Liszt. And as a matter of fact the best parts of *Pénélope* are those which approximate to the older conception of an aria. There is, for instance, Penelope's apostrophe to the absent Ulysses, sung over the same music previously employed for the dance, commanded as a diversion by the Suitors and very much akin in its turn to the traditional ballet interlude:

[1] *Opinions musicales de Gabriel Fauré*, ed. Gheusi, p. 125.

There is also the song of the old swineherd Eumæus which opens Act II with a rhythm recalling the seventh Nocturne; it is better, I think, than another page of music-drama almost contemporary with it, the Old Harper's song in Rutland Boughton's *Immortal Hour*, which bears a certain resemblance to it in mood and relevance, and which also owes much of its virtue to the fact that it is in essence an aria, with an individual independence of its own. The part of Eumæus is indeed in some ways the most satisfactory in the opera; not only has he thus to strike the prevailing note of the second act, but he is given in the third, just before the scene where the suitors try Ulysses' bow, one of the finest passages of pure recitative:

And though the final scene of all is rather like a concession to a different kind of convention, as Mr. Copland noted:

> Particularly the last scene, with its tableau of Penelope and Ulysses surrounded by the chorus of shepherds singing the usual 'Gloire à Zeus', seems a stupidly operatic finish that might easily have been avoided. But other operas have survived in spite of their librettos, and so will this one.[1]

yet in justice to Fauchois it should be pointed out that this ending apparently formed no part of the original plan, but was demanded by the director of the Monte Carlo theatre in order (as Fauré bitterly remarked) 'to replace the peaceful ending by a lot of noise and fuss'.[2]

Pénélope, vastly superior though it is to a whole range of popular favourites in opera with whose melodrama and catchiness it makes no attempt to compete, is thus not sure enough of its own direction to be a supreme masterpiece. But it has a place in the history of French culture as a representative work on the musical side of French neo-Hellenism. Derogatory comparisons with Parisian drawing-rooms notwithstanding, it seems to me that Fauré's generation and its successors (Anatole France, for example, who was a year his senior and died within a few weeks of him) interpreted Greece for the modern world better than many people elsewhere who insisted on the primitive features of the Greek archaic period. To those for whom *Prométhée* was not violent enough as a translation of Aeschylus, *Pénélope* will fall short of the starkness they imagine for Homer. The seductiveness of the spinning-chorus and the flute-players' dance in Act I, the almost idyllic setting of Act II with its wistful moonlight dialogue on a hill overlooking the sea—these things, they will say, belong rather to the atmosphere imported into the Homeric legend by an elaborate modern civilization. And yet, what do such critics imagine to be the value of the legacy of Greece to modern times, or, for that matter, the value of Homer to the leading spirits of the best Greek period? What

[1] *The Musical Quarterly* (New York), October 1924.

[2] P. Fauré-Fremiet, *op. cit.*, p. 78.

would Homer have meant to Sophocles or Plato had these latter writers considered themselves debarred from supplementing him by the more highly evolved civilization of their own epoch? The reason why modern Europeans return ceaselessly to a Greek inspiration is precisely the example set by Greece—in proportion as it was most Hellenic in the flower of its Attic phase—of civilized living and a civilized outlook on life. True that in the age of the Rococo it had been a common error to treat the Greek mentality as though it were expressed solely in the luxurious refinements of Hellenistic Alexandria; but a much graver error was committed by those researchers of the nineteenth century, whose posterity is with us yet, and to whom the Hellenic type was to be found in the semi-barbarities of Dorian Sparta, while they conspired to present the Homeric poems as specimens of primitive minstrelsy, a little more than *Beowulf* and less than the Sagas. This was another of the aberrations of romanticism, from which as from many others the recovery was earliest and most conclusively to be perceived among French thinkers. Anatole France was one of the first to hold the 'primitivistic' idea of Homer up to ridicule, as was recognized by Charles Maurras, himself the author of a notable protest against 'the forcible incorporation of Homer into Mycenean barbarism'.[1] Admittedly the almost decadent 'Alexandrian' culture was not of a piece with the classical purity of Attic Greece; but it is a nearer road to the understanding of it than any cult of archaic crudity could be; and this may help to explain how Fauré's previous experiences with the sensual richness of *Caligula*, or with the 'Latin charm'[2] of such songs as *La Rose*, helped rather than hindered him to a clear and balanced apprehension of the Hellenic subjects on which he was later to try his strength.

[1] *Anthinéa*, p. 54. Maurras, born some twenty-three years later than Fauré, began as a very illuminating writer on the Grecophil theme, and I make no apology for quoting him here; his questionable influence through the *Action française*, and his recent record as a near-collaborator with the Germans, do not invalidate the insight he displayed in 1901 as an interpreter of classical Hellas.

[2] As M. Koechlin called it: *op. cit.*, p. 50.

Pénélope is a sophisticated, not a naïve product; but it is not any less accurate a guide to classical antiquity for that.

Fauré made his own position on this matter fairly clear in the course of a review, written in 1921, of Berlioz's *Troyens à Carthage*, which he described as 'enveloped in an atmosphere of calm, nobility and serene beauty such as could not fail to be created in that poetic mind by contact with Greek antiquity'; adding almost immediately that 'this was "Mediterranean music" long before Nietzsche had given that name to certain other musical productions of this country'[1]. Evidently he saw no incongruity between classical Greece and the voluptuous south; and one is only a little surprised at the example he chose for bringing them together. The explanation is partly that he regarded the *Troyens* as something of an exception in the work of Berlioz, whom he regretfully admitted in the same review to have had 'a brain and a heart in which everything took on excessive proportions'; and though he did all the justice in his power to the other compositions of a writer whose disregard of the 'classical principle of measure' argued an ideal so different from his own, yet there were times when this sense of fairness felt strained to parting. Of Berlioz' *Requiem* he could say no more than that it was 'a work in which a taste for big dramatic effects, and an indifference towards what concerns religious music —or, for that matter, music pure and simple—may find equal satisfaction', noting ironically that the orchestra was 'reinforced for the occasion with two score brass instruments, six pairs of kettledrums, two bass drums, gong and cymbals, *ad majorem Dei gloriam*'.[2]

Fauré's own *Requiem* might almost be an answer to this type of music, for it is scored—in addition to the soprano and baritone solos and the choir in four, occasionally divided to six parts—for violas and violoncellos *divisi*, supported by double-basses and the organ playing a kind of *continuo* part, with horns and trumpets in a few sharply defined entries, a harp in three only of the seven movements, and no other strings except a single violin solo for

[1] *Opinions musicales*, pp. 22-3. [2] *Ibid.*, p. 21.

the *Sanctus*; the distribution of the string parts half-anticipating that of Stravinsky's *Psalm-Symphony*. But whereas Stravinsky's motive in dispensing with both violins and violas was presumably an austere avoidance of the caressing tone which he could not hope otherwise to eliminate, the effect of Fauré's scoring is to match the funerary purpose of his work with the restrained though not gloomy expressiveness that comes of a sparing use of upper frequencies.

The *Requiem* is what hardly any of the great composers' masses had been in the century elapsing since Mozart—it is suited to the liturgical use, and does not ask to be a concert work. And moreover it neither limits itself by dispensing with part of the musical language available for secular compositions, like the English Victorians, nor does it sound inappropriate by using it, like the church music of Rossini. A great many of Fauré's other liturgical pieces, especially his solo anthems, follow a Gounodian type which he surpasses only because he was a greater composer than Gounod, not by any essential departure from the model; but here we have a work which is as much a part of his radical revitalizing of French music as any of the songs and chamber works. For the *Requiem* illustrates as well Fauré's use of the refertilizing force latent in the 'Gregorian' modes as his mastery of unpretentious innovations in musical language; and, further, it is a standing proof that these two features are but facets of the same thing. The main theme of the *Introit*

is of a kind familiar enough to us now, but must have given even greater offence to the conventional sensibilities of the 1880s than a similar passage in the death scene of *Boris Godunov*:

since, whereas Mussorgsky merely allowed himself the flat seventh of the true minor mode, Fauré used it in conjunction with the triad of the third degree (the F major chord in the key of D minor) regarded by timid theorists as having no place in a correct progression.[1] The other side of the picture is provided by the canonic subject of the *Offertorium*, converging as it does on a perfect example of Fauré's new discoveries with chords of the seventh; the organ and strings enter with a sliding series of three of them—the 'leading', 'dominant' and 'minor' sevenths—at the end of the canon:

the same point of the text, be it noted, where Mozart also had introduced surprising effects of harmonic resolution; and it is

[1] It is still so regarded by textbooks of harmony in our own time.

also by means of two chords of the seventh, one 'major' and one 'leading', that the orchestra makes its most telling commentary on the almost monotoned chant given to the solo baritone for 'Hostias et preces tibi'.

The next movement, *Sanctus*, in which a few simple phrases are sung in unison over a semiquaver figure on the harp, while the solo violin weaves a descant above them, carries us again into the elegiac atmosphere of Fauré's 'autumnal' or 'crepuscular' songs. It is the *Sanctus* of a Requiem and not of a High Mass for general purposes; the entry of the brass at 'Hosanna in excelsis' is not so much an interruption of the elegiac tone as a confirmation of it by stronger powers—after which the original material is resumed, the violin solo now sounding like a gentle spirit going to its rest. There is no *Benedictus*; its place is taken by the last two lines (*Pie Jesu*) of the Sequence for the Dead, the rest of which Fauré did not set either, so that his work provides no opportunity for comparison with the eschatological eloquence of the *Dies iræ* and *Tuba mirum* in other Requiem Masses.[1] This *Pie Jesu* is for soprano solo, and its intense pathos derives not from vocal strenuousness but from just the reverse; the voice moves mostly in intervals of a tone or a minor third, and its effect is enhanced by a similar movement reflected in the lower strings and harp:

The *Agnus Dei* is another instance of descant treatment: it is sung (mostly by the tenors) to the accompaniment of a counter-

[1] Mlle. Nadia Boulanger made a curious error here; she wrote (in the *Revue musicale* for October 1922) of 'un doux *Benedictus*', and could only have been referring to the *Pie Jesu*.

melody which, by its drop of a sixth near the beginning and its tumble down the arpeggio just before the end, is strangely suggestive of Elgar (compare the trombone entry in his first Symphony, coda of first movement):

To the *Agnus* is added, as usual, the Communion *Lux æterna*, sung by full choir; after which there returns the melody for strings, quoted above, no longer in the *relative* major (F) but in the *tonic* major (D), thus constituting a kind of provisional close. For the remaining two movements are not taken from the text of the Mass for the Dead, but from that of the Order of Burial. One, the Responsorium *Libera me* (sung for the absolution of the deceased in those Requiem Masses which are prefatory to burial), is a powerful extended melody bridging once and for all that gulf between sacred and secular music which has never been very wide in the estimation of great composers; and in the course of it there occurs the only passage of Fauré's work which may be thought to compensate in some sort for the absence of a *Dies iræ* setting. The other is the antiphon *In Paradisum*, which has points in common (beyond the D major tonality) with the Angel's Farewell in *Gerontius*, but with a difference: its serenity is not troubled by questionings like those expressed in Elgar's male-chorus entry, and with its quiet harp figure and low-registered chords for the choir it concludes the *Requiem* on a note of calm—not even of hope—which impelled P. Tinel to suggest that it should rather be headed *In Elysium*.

Which raises the question, frequently debated since the appearance of the *Requiem*—is it rather pagan than Christian in tone? Certainly, Fauré's choice of sections of the text is a little unusual, though not unprecedented. Other Requiem Masses have ended with the *Libera me*—Verdi's, for example—and the sixteenth-century Spanish composer Victoria wrote one which not only included this responsorium but, like Fauré's, omitted the *Dies iræ*.[1] Fauré's *Requiem*, however, is perhaps, more than any other, a Requiem without the Last Judgment; the terrors of the after-life are hardly more than touched upon, and the untroubled mood of the *In Paradisum* differs from *Gerontius* precisely by an absence of any notion of Purgatory. M. Jean Chantavoine described the work as 'a paradisiacal imagining, with no trace of torment or of doubt, scarcely even of mourning'[2] —an overstatement of a case which Tinel put rather better by characterizing it as 'fadeless serenity', adding: 'Were not the ancients our masters in the art of wedding essentially voluptuous ideas to funereal thoughts?'; which throws into relief a prominent element of the *Requiem*, its evocation of the comforting rather than the exigent aspect which men have from time to time read upon the face of death. Comforting, but not 'sheltering'; it was written at the most dejected period of his life, but I do not find in it any attempt to seek the consolations of religion for his own sorrows. Neither can I accept the romantic rather than convincing theory of Camille Bellaigue[3] that he was singing a dirge in it upon his lost love for Marianne Viardot. That episode, in so far as it affected his music, had been exorcised by the *adagio* of the first Quartet and by the *Élégie* which so resembles it—both, it will be noted, are in C minor and end with a pianoforte melody over a semiquaver figure supported by a pedal-point in the violoncello part—works in which the same personal trace had also been found by his friend Mme. Clerc.[4] No, the *Requiem* represents neither effusion nor conversion, but rather the unperturbed vision of one whose attention was just then fixed on death, since it was then that he lost his parents. And this is doubtless what Camille Benoît, first among many, had detected

[1] Gilbert Chase, *The Music of Spain*, p. 83.

[2] *Le Ménestrel*, 16th June 1922.

[3] Introduction to the letters in the *Revue des Deux Mondes*, 15th August 1928.

[4] P. Fauré-Fremiet, *op. cit.*, p. 42.

when he drew a parallel to Fauré from the neo-Hellenic, non-Christian sympathies of the 'Parnassian' poets, illustrating it with a number of quotations from Anatole France's poetic drama, *Les Noces corinthiennes*.

This attribution was however hotly contested by M. Philippe Fauré-Fremiet, who was anxious to claim the work as imbued with a sense of mystery and full of faith in a forgiving God. He wrote in 1928, in the full tide of a religious reaction against French Hellenism as represented in Anatole France and other typical contemporaries of his father; the movement to deny the discerning reason its right to control human affairs had been growing for some years, for the 'Parnassian' sense of human dignity (the first attempt at anything of its kind since the collapse of values in romanticism) had threatened to expose such a variety of intellectual insufficiencies that it could hardly fail to become unpopular, and Philippe Fauré could not endure that the *Requiem* should suffer from this unpopularity. His own description of the work, in places, causes it indeed to accord more closely with the outlook, unobstructed by mystical astigmatism, of an Anatole France than he himself suspected: 'It comes about that Fauré, unwilling to describe heaven, yet gives us a glimpse of it, because . . . he has eliminated from prayer its passionate element—that is, terror'.[1] But for the most part the pages he has devoted to this central masterpiece—on which, more than on any other of the large-scale works, Fauré's reputation depends—are, in both senses of the word, pious; and his well-meant efforts on the whole do more harm than otherwise to his father's fame. They offer such a handle to the perpetuation of the 'Fauré legend'—that of a composer whose charm was allied to weakness—that one thinks of the similar legend of a 'gentle' Delius, sedulously circulated until Mr. Eric Fenby revealed beyond a doubt the acridly undevout character of his late employer.

Not of course that Fauré's mass inclines to the type of a 'Pagan Requiem' as Delius used the term; for the very reason that 'earth-worship' was as foreign to his outlook as any other

[1] *Op. cit.*, p. 50.

mysticism. He represents the urbane enlightenment of France in the most adult phases of her culture, for which metaphysical principles, no less than Christian dogmas, had to be purged of superstition[1] before they were acceptable; not those regrettable interludes of her history given over to a naïve glorification of the 'innocent' and the 'subconscious'. Even his evocations of childhood, such as *Dolly*, are no more naïve, though less ironic, than Debussy's; the single exception to this statement, the song *En prière* (written for a publisher's venture, a collection by various composers, called *Contes mystiques*) is significantly a failure. There was nothing of the wide-eyed child about Fauré, nor of the willing slave of the irrational; just as in poetry it was Leconte de Lisle and the Parnassians who rescued him when he had lost his way with Hugo, so in general critical thought his equivalent is rather Maurras (of the Grecophil period) than Bergson. His son, while insisting that he was not a sceptic, admits nevertheless that he was not devout[2]; and we may best understand (and admire the more) his religious standpoint by remembering that he once wrote a 'profane' work, a *Madrigal* for small choir (Op. 35) to an amatory text by the joyous sensualist Armand Silvestre, in which he thought nc harm to use a theme resembling the chorale famous in Bach as 'Aus tiefer Not schrei' ich zu Dir', ironically adapted from the implorings of prayer to the implorings of love:

Death, then, as a comforter rather than a summoner; as a curtain descending upon life rather than a fulfilment of it; as the sleep for which Macbeth longed after life's fitful fever, rather than the entrance to a world of new strenuousness where they rest not day nor night; all this seems to me to be conveyed by the illusionless tranquillity of Fauré's *Requiem*. Its out-

[1] And by the term 'superstition' I mean the moral kind, so much more pernicious than the material.

[2] P. Fauré-Fremiet, *op. cit.*, p. 49.

standing distinction from many other Masses for the Dead is perhaps the prominence it gives to the word *requiem* itself, which appears in all but two of the seven movements, is thrown into strong relief wherever it occurs, and forms not only the first but also the last word in the work—the fact that it enabled Fauré to end with the word *requiem* may have been one reason for his choosing the Antiphon *In Paradisum* to set as a concluding section, and it is moreover noteworthy that the only lines (*Pie Jesu*) which he used from the Sequence (*Dies iræ*) centre upon the same word, to which Fauré even added the extra-liturgical 'sempiternam' by way of underlining his meaning. Not only pious terrors, but false hopes, are absent from his scheme; which may be said to render the *Requiem* all the more suitable for a mourning as distinct from a mystical purpose. Rest, eternal rest—is not this an idea of death which one will entertain all the more in proportion as one has 'warmed both hands before the fire of life'?[1] Our immortality is in our memory, the message seems to be from those songs written on the threshold of Fauré's own dissolution:

which complement the *Requiem* with a Greek sense of consummation. Nowhere was his art more Hellenic, wrote M. Koechlin, than in 'the primordial value that it found in this human life of ours'[2]—of which, furthermore, it was part of the Greek wisdom to enthrone the arts as the main consolation and on which they, more than any other object of human reverence, bestow an ultimate significance; as was stated with a certain poetic finality in one of the writings of Maurras, an ode to

[1] W. S. Landor. [2] *Op. cit.*, p. 194.

Pallas, goddess of the arts, quoted by Mlle. Nadia Boulanger as eminently appropriate to the case of Fauré:

> Thy servant may share in that which is beyond time. His very exertions shall achieve grace by their ease, and his very pleasures be virtuous because of their nobility. . . . The man whom thou consolest may abandon himself to the fleeting hour and not feel its sting.[1]

That which best makes use of time shall most surely be beyond time; and having used and enjoyed it, we may rest.

> Gabriel Fauré one day quoted Saint-Évremond[2]: 'The love of pleasure, and the avoidance of pain, are the first and most natural impulses observable in mankind.' And he added: 'Art has therefore every reason to be voluptuous.' . . . Here was his glory: to have discovered new sound-forms which set free our hearts and our senses, and do not debase them.[3]

He was of the company of Bach, Mozart and Debussy, the last-named of whom also 'admired the inherent sensuousness'[4] of the first; a sensuousness which 'did not prevent them from writing in a pure style, from knowing how to construct, from evoking deep feelings'.[5] And this, as it typified the art of the Hellenes, entered also into the music Fauré wrote to accompany the dead on their last journey, as into his other works; for he knew that it is when a life has been savoured without inhibition that it will most satisfactorily close.

[1] *La Revue musicale*, October 1922 (from the article on Fauré's church music; quoting Maurras, *Invocation à Minerve* from *L'Avenir de l'Intelligence*).

[2] An Epicurean writer of the generation of Molière and La Fontaine.

[3] Georges Auric, in the *Revue musicale* for December 1924.

[4] E. Lockspeiser, *Debussy*, p. 193.

[5] Koechlin, *op. cit.*, p. 182.

CHAPTER VIII

CONCLUSIONS AND GENERALITIES

ONE of Fauré's most appreciative critics in his own country wrote, as early as January 1910:

> If in recent years French music has been given a different orientation and, so to say, adopted new habits, it is to Gabriel Fauré that the honour is due.[1]

To us in England the 'new habits' were made known before we were very well acquainted with their 'onlie begetter'. It was not until the 1914 war that English audiences were given much chance of understanding that there was something in French music beyond the operas *Faust*, *Carmen* and *Samson et Dalila* and the pianoforte pieces of Cécile Chaminade; and when the news was brought, the names most prominent in the headlines were those of Fauré's juniors, chiefly Debussy and Ravel. The first edition of *Dolly* (1893) had been published in London, and Fauré had conducted his own *Pelléas* music at the Prince of Wales Theatre; but it was many years before the knowledge of him in this country extended much beyond a bare realization of the fact that there was such a thing as the *mélodie* as well as the *Lied*. His *Requiem*, for example, was not performed in London until 1936[2]. Those of us, however, who were fortunate enough to be introduced to his works at the same time as those of his pupils and successors will remember that his music, no less than theirs, came to us as a deliverance, to an extent which had scarcely been the case even with Wagner and beside which the self-consciously advertised 'music of the future', as the post-Wagnerians understood it, pales into insignificance. At last it was made evident to us that a great deal of what we had hitherto believed to be the centre and the norm of music was in reality nothing but German music. How neces-

[1] J. Saint-Jean, in *La Nouvelle Revue*, Vol. XIII, p. 256.

[2] Robert Elkin, *Queen's Hall*, p. 65.

sary this deliverance was may be understood by those who also remember that even a composer of such comparatively small though genuine importance as Grieg produced, to a lesser degree, the same effect. The Russians had also helped in our liberation; but it was the French composers who did most to break the yoke; and a share may thus be claimed for Fauré in the process by which a whole generation of our own composers, in the early part of the present century, availed themselves of the French example to write again—for the first time since more than a century—music worthy of their country's older achievements.

This was more especially true as concerned song-writing; whereas in his own country Fauré was a pioneer of modernity on more general lines, and moreover 'not simply a precursor, a pioneer whose path was widened by better-equipped explorers, but a musician who spoke fluently in a prophetic language a quarter of a century before other composers'.[1] The author of this remark had made one very like it a dozen years earlier: 'The boldest explorers everywhere find the footprints of M. Fauré, who—without haste or self-advertisement—has travelled over all their wonderland before them.'[2]

What tended to make his discoveries less immediately noticeable was the fact that they were mainly in the syntax rather than the vocabulary of musical language. His innovations were of the opposite kind from those, for example, of Scriabin, who was concerned chiefly to exploit harmonic combinations hitherto unfamiliar in themselves; Fauré tended rather to strike out fresh ways of passing from one harmony to another. There is a parallel fact about his melody, which appears at its most characteristic in long-stretching lines, supported by his recurrent rhythms and continuous figuration, as we have seen in a variety of his compositions ranging from the first two chamber works, through the melodies for the *Agnus* and the *Libera me* of the *Requiem*, to such crowns of his endeavour as the second Quintet; whereas in contrast the melodic style of Franck (to quote another

[1] E. Vuillermoz in the *Revue musicale*, October 1922.

[2] In *Musica*, February 1909; quoted by Séré, *Musiciens français d'aujourd'hui*, p. 191.

fruitful spirit who, though a score of years his senior, was as a composer his contemporary) concentrates attention especially on intensely charged moments. Fauré also has these moments, but they are usually such as to illuminate the larger structure, whereas Franck's outlines more often seem to exist for the sake of them. The result of all this is to give a peculiar homogeneity to Fauré's style, in which Vincent d'Indy also observed that 'musical invention assumes a very special character, which we may call melodico-harmonic, for his melody seems so bound up with his subtle harmonies that it cannot be considered apart from them'.[1] His inventiveness in this double direction is mainly a matter of the developments he brought about in the too-long-restricted syntax of music that he found at his disposal.

This, as bequeathed to the early and mid-nineteenth century from the age of Beethoven, was somewhat of a depleted inheritance. In the time of Purcell and Alessandro Scarlatti, and even a generation later with J. S. Bach, music still remembered the modes, though the reign of the more limited diatonicism was beginning; and hence it was possible to treat chords otherwise than with the notion of a leading-note or a perfect cadence always just round the corner, or nearer. But the result of another century of Italo-German collaboration was to establish a system of harmony whereby all compound sonorities were to be judged according as they were susceptible of resolution into triads, with as near the effect of a dominant-to-tonic progression as possible; so that in the 1850s, except where a feeling for modality had been kept alive—or revived—the study of harmonic successions was practically restricted to those depending either on the perfect cadence or on the resolution of dominant and diminished sevenths, with an occasional concession to another chord of a strong leading-note flavour, the augmented (or 'extreme sharp') sixth. The remaining chords of the seventh, no doubt for the very reason that they do not lend themselves so readily to resolution of this uniform kind, did not receive the same attention, or were treated, along with the ninth and other complex chords, as suspensions. The value of Rameau's system of building by thirds

[1] *Cours de composition musicale*, Bk. II; quoted by Séré, *op. cit.*, p. 188.

may be seen to have lain partly in the fact that it invited a consideration of sevenths, ninths and the rest on their own merits as independently existing harmonic compounds; but the authority followed throughout the 'Viennese period'—and beyond—was not Rameau, whom Marpurg also had supported in this matter, but Fux[1], whose system as continued by Albrechtsberger lay at the root of most Italian and German work of that very romantic period whose practitioners most affected to despise it. Even Schumann tended to treat his 'minor' and 'leading' sevenths, and all higher compounds, as suspensions only; the real deliverance was to come when the progression to and from these chords could normally be made in such a way as to suggest neither a cadence nor a resolved suspension but a line of independent direction.

The 'leading seventh' was the first chord to be liberated in this way. Wagner's is the name of central importance here; for he (still more than Tchaikovsky, with whom the chord was a favourite but who usually resolved it upon the dominant or the tonic harmony of the minor key) based some of his finest passages on strikingly original motions to or from a leading seventh or one of its inversions[2]. With Wagner the root of this chord is very seldom employed as a leading-note. Fauré operated the same deliverance for other chords of the seventh, especially the 'minor' and 'major' sevenths, the latter of which was a frequent element of his originality, particularly when he used it 'unprepared':

É - changent des propos fa - des sous les ra-mu - - res

[1] W. S. Rockstro, *Practical Harmony*, p. 65, n.

[2] Examples occur to me from *Götterdämmerung*: in the scene known as 'Hagen's Watch' and at a point in the closing scene where Brünnhilde calls for a pyre to be built.

FAURÉ'S PIANO AND PORTRAIT OF SARGENT

And the triads themselves have reason to be grateful to him for a renewed freedom of syntactic association, which they enjoy by virtue of his having applied to modern music his familiarity with the ancient modes; so that when he harmonized a Hymn to Apollo discovered by the French School at Athens the result was not unlike his original compositions. His harmony was, in fact, 'fluid enough to accept the classic formulæ of syllogism in sound, without ever becoming their slave'.[1]

It frequently happens that a practice deriving from the harmony implicit in one of the modes is precisely what accounts for the 'modernity' of Fauré's writing. Foremost among such practices is that of dispensing with the leading-note and its too emphatic[2] pointing towards the tonic of a scale, as also with other items of musical syntax based on a similar principle, and thus avoiding the 'dead level of major' which so wearied Hopkins[3]. Successive applications of this method may be traced through an early but mature work, the C minor piano Quartet. In the two extracts from its first movement quoted in Chapter V[4] we may observe, first a subject whose melodic flat seventh is matched by the harmony of the 'forbidden' third degree—as in the Introit of the *Requiem*[5]—and secondly a transformation of this subject so as to centre on a chord of the ninth which not only contains a flat seventh but omits the third belonging to the traditional dominant-ninth chord, all of which eliminates any suggestion of a leading-note either in the initial tonality (E flat) or in the progression towards the next (A flat). In the trio of the Scherzo a similar comment is invited by the flattening of two degrees of the scale for its melody:

while the opening bars of the *Adagio* are remarkable for a significant point—marked (a) in the extract—at which the E flat

[1] Jean Chantavoine in the *Ménestrel* for 14th November 1924.

[2] I am indebted to M. Koechlin (*op. cit.*, p. 159) for this identification of the vice latent in 'leading' semitones.

[3] See p. 54. [4] See pp. 91-2. [5] See pp. 172-3.

of the harmony, forming an inversion of the *minor* seventh where E natural would have produced a *dominant* seventh, not only fulfils the condition for 'modulation' in Hopkins's rather than the 'tempered' sense, but also serves in a curious way to sustain the elegiac dignity of the movement:

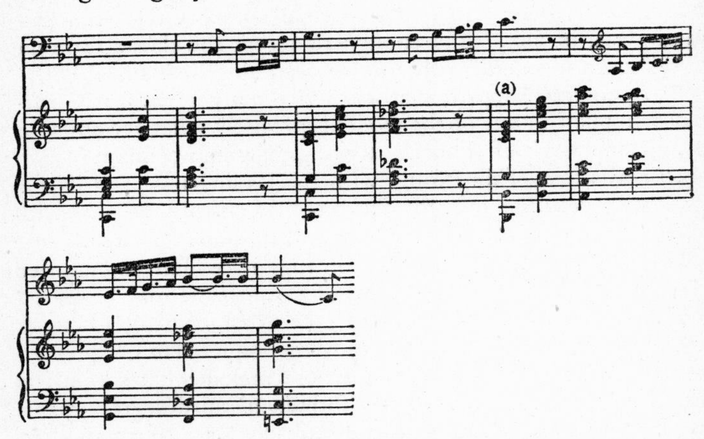

And these modal-sounding flat intervals continued to be at the basis of much of Fauré's invention throughout the period of his accomplishment; as in this from the *Bonne Chanson*:

It is moreover the avoidance of 'leading' semitones which accounts for his characteristic variation on the plagal cadence; one example of which occurs at the end of a line quoted in

Chapter IV from *La Rose*[1], while others a little better known may be found in the second subject of the *Masques et bergamasques* Overture and (with the first chord of the cadence one inversion higher) in the *Sicilienne*:

There is no need to emphasize any further Fauré's indebtedness in this respect to his Niedermeyer training; nor to enquire deeply into the possibility that his modal tendency was encouraged by the similar cast of French folk-music[2]—except to note in passing that of all European folksong it is the Italian and German, especially the latter, which comes nearest to our established idea of a major scale with a tonic-and-dominant scaffolding, so that the break with this scale-system might be expected to come from elsewhere than either of these two nationalities, as in fact it did.[3]

The use made by Fauré of these ancient forms of musical speech consisted more particularly in a development of them along lines different from those followed in the course of musical history[4]; he went back as it were to the fork of the roads and took the other turning, and indeed travelled so far along it as to be able to see those of his companions whom he had left on the more familiar road. We have observed above, and elsewhere,[5] his fondness for cadential progressions of a 'plagal' affinity; another of them:

[1] See pp. 80-1.

[2] As M. Koechlin suggests; *op. cit.*, p. 158, n.

[3] Incidentally it was this element of French music, as well as of the Russian music where the modes had never been forgotten, that helped to render the example of both so fruitful in England, whose folk-music is similarly almost innocent of the major scale.

[4] See p. 69.

[5] See p. 127.

2nd Piano Quartet, Op. 45.

may serve to remind us of the prominent part played in his work by another turn of phrase rejected in the earlier evolution of music: the tritone. This, whether in its melodic form or as a 'false relation', has already been shown to have given the unmistakable flavour to a great many of Fauré's works[1]; and it only remains for me now, in order to complete my necessarily rapid account of the matter, to point out first how he gave it a fresh meaning each time he used it—one instance from the second violin Sonata bears a resemblance (though at a greater speed) to a phrase in Elgar's second Symphony, which he certainly could never have heard:

—and then to call attention to a constantly recurring feature of his later works which I can only describe as a tritonic *appoggiatura*:

[1] See pp. 62 and 146

these examples of which, marked (a), from the *Andante* of the same Sonata, may be read in conjunction with the extract from the eighth Barcarolle in Chapter VI[1] and with the thematic references to the *Fantaisie*, Op. 111, in the same chapter. Nor does this begin to exhaust the list; the later song-cycles and the string Quartet are full of these *appoggiature* in which an augmented fourth narrows to a major third. Something like the same process in the reverse order is to be found in the harmony widening to or from a major seventh, of which an illustration has been given in Chapter IV from the *Mirages*[2] and another is provided by the *Fantaisie* (Op. 79) for flute and piano, where it appears first as follows:

and then in Fauré's usual broken figuration:

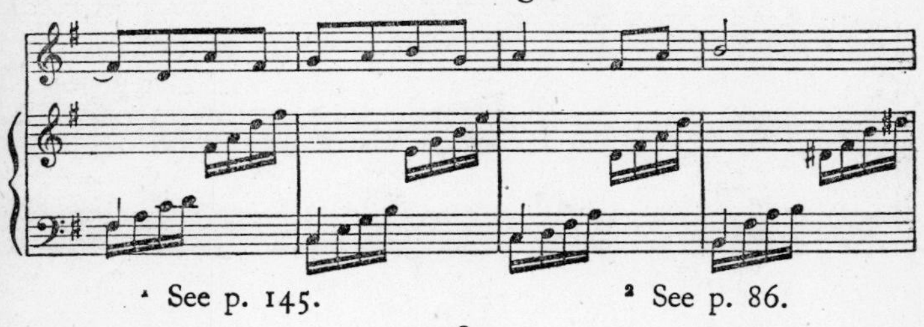

[1] See p. 145. [2] See p. 86.

Putting all this together with other opportunities inherent in his 'rich keyboard', which had no special relation to possibilities undeveloped by older schools but were merely waiting until the bonds of tonic and dominant were broken asunder and the cords of the leading-note cast away, one may form some idea of the wide range of musical expression at Fauré's disposal. I refer my readers to a line quoted in Chapter IV from *La fleur qui va sur l'eau*[1], which exemplifies the suppleness of his constructions in that a note at any place in the texture is liable to become a suspension almost as soon as it appears; I may also complement a number of previous references to the augmented triad by observing at how early a date Fauré availed himself of the tonal ambiguities of this chord, in the second pianoforte Quartet:

It is unnecessary to repeat at greater length with what mastery he carried the enharmonic principle to still further degrees of subtlety, except to point out the value of the flexibility thus achieved for his sequential writing (*La Bonne Chanson*):

[1] See p. 82.

a feature of his style which might easily have become wearisome were it not that, as his career progressed, he was increasingly careful to use only ideas of rich quality for his sequences[1]:

1st Violoncello Sonata.

And lastly it should be noted how this flexibility was ever more apparent in what I have several times described as his easy recovery of tonalities: that 'grace as of a cat falling on its feet', of which a hint had been given as early as the *Cantique de Racine*, and of which I cannot forbear quoting one more example, from the *Andante* of the Trio written nearly sixty years later:

[1] See pp. 98 and 134; also Koechlin, *op. cit.*, p. 173 and n.

Fauré's work may with some propriety be divided, as it has become the custom to do with every possible composer of note since Beethoven, into three periods; though Louis Vuillemin[1] tried to make it four—misled, I think, by the publication of his songs in those three convenient volumes before there was any question of the *Chanson d'Ève* and the remaining albums. I prefer to think of his career as divided into apprenticeship, maturity and further exploration, with the inevitable overlapping between the periods; the two chamber works Opp. 13 and 15 being, for instance, more mature than the three Nocturnes Op. 33 or the comparatively inconsiderable *Poème d'un jour*[2]. The first period, therefore, extending perhaps to about 1884 (which was the date of his discarded Symphony, Op. 40), contains much that may not by any right be called 'prentice-work'—songs such as *Nell* and *Les Berceaux*, and the *Élégie*, as well as the first Sonata and first Quartet—but throughout these years his pianoforte writing was a little inclined to follow Chopin and Mendelssohn in their *salon* manner, his songs were liable to fall back towards Gounod (partly because he had not yet learned to distinguish unerringly between the more and the less profitable among the poems that presented themselves to him for setting) and he was still making uncertain ventures at the symphonic style. The next line of demarcation should probably be drawn somewhere between his appointment as professor at the Conservatoire and the composition of *Prométhée*; the second period will thus take in the second Quartet, the *Requiem*, the

[1] *Gabriel Fauré et son œuvre*, p. 15.

[2] Three songs, Op. 21, to words by Charles Grandmougin (who also supplied the text for Franck's *Hulda*).

Verlaine songs and a number of pianoforte works culminating in the magnificent seventh Nocturne of 1898. The line is difficult to draw for the additional reason that between the works belonging recognizably to the second and to the third period there is something of an interregnum; it is almost as though for the first time in his life Fauré had found it necessary to measure his own stature by conscious comparison with German music. Often enough he had been called 'the French Schumann'; Vuillemin, writing in 1913, repeated the parallel by pairing the two Quartets with Schumann's chamber music and the *Bonne Chanson* with the *Dichterliebe*[1]; and certainly the *Variations*, by the disposition of their part-writing as well as the similitude of key, are to some extent a homage to the *Études symphoniques*. Fauré had also by this time, it would seem, become rather more apprehensively aware of the imposing presence of Wagner; in the writing of *Prométhée* his awareness no doubt took the form of a deliberate avoidance of Wagnerian imitation as far as in him lay, but this was already a contrast to the confidence of his youth when, even though full of admiration for Wagner and with the avowed intention of emulating the forest scene in *Siegfried*, he produced in earnest of his endeavour the *Ballade*, than which no music was ever less marked by the Wagnerian stamp[2]. Towards Brahms he was, like most Frenchmen, quite unsympathetic—in 1904 he even applied to the E minor Symphony the epithets 'dull' and 'redundant'[3]—and therefore ran no danger of losing his way in attendance upon a master from whom, even had he better recognized his genius, he had nothing to learn; but his immunity in this respect did not extend far enough back in musical history, since, as we have seen, even while thus publicly disowning Brahms he was engaged on the completion of his first Quintet in a manner too evidently inspired by the less happy promptings of Beethoven.

Fortunately the deviation did not last long nor take him too far out of his true way, and the third period (which may be

[1] *Op. cit.*, pp. 49 and 33.
[2] J. Saint-Jean, *loc. cit.*, p. 271; see also Koechlin, *op. cit.*, p. 81, n.
[3] *Opinions musicales*, p. 26.

dated with rough convenience from the time when Heugel began to publish for him) is as notable for the new ground he broke as the second had been for the increased fertility he had imparted to the old. His works now inclined more and more towards tenuity of texture—even *Pénélope*, substantial though it may seem as against Debussy, has only to be compared with the operas of Richard Strauss for the justice of my observation to be immediately apparent—while at the same time the direction of each line in his scores became even more significant than before. This revised method—when it does not express itself in pure monody such as that of *Diane*, *Sélèné*—may perhaps be illustrated by placing it alongside the counterpoint of Bach in contrast to that of Wagner. Comparing the second violin Sonata with the first, it will be seen that the greater spareness of the later work almost obliges each part of the polyphonic structure to charge itself more highly, so that even the indispensable quaver or semiquaver figuration of Fauré's pianoforte writing assumes an additional function like that of the passage-work of Bach, which similarly contributes to the design and not only to the motion of his music. Fauré, it would seem, had been waiting to achieve mastery in this kind of writing before finally dispensing with the pianoforte, hitherto the inseparable companion of his finest inspirations, and composing a string Quartet; in which he presents something of a contrast to Franck, whose Quartet was also the work of his old age, but who wrote for the medium in a way not essentially different from that which he had previously adopted for the organ or the orchestra. The purity of line in Fauré's Quartet and other chamber works of this period, making no concessions to merely 'effective' instrumentation; the unadulterated musicality of such a song-cycle as *L'Horizon chimérique*, relentlessly banishing *portamento* and all other tricks of vocalization; the intense austerity of the later Barcarolles and Nocturnes into which one would hesitate for very shame to import *rubato* or any other adjunct of expressive superficiality—all this combines to announce one of the classic composers of a latter age, on whom our own century may look back with reverent indebtedness. As Jean Chantavoine wrote:

'Though at times it seemed that he was to be classed as a "Decadent"[1], he has remained a classic—or will become one.'

A modern classic in that his work will be increasingly recognized as having established the principles which give a meaning to that of his successors—in this respect my only quarrel with a judgment of Georges Auric is that it claims *too little* for him; is it not true, asked Auric, that by his example we were 'prepared for the great revelation brought about by Debussy? Can we ever hope to reckon how many, as a result of knowing and loving his *paysage choisi*[2], were more readily appreciative of the magic of *Pelléas*?'[3] This is doubtless true, but it makes Fauré into too much of a precursor and too little of an artist of primary importance; it needs to be complemented by a consideration of the long line of his pupils and successors to whom Debussy's revelation was in great measure the news of discoveries some at least of which Fauré had already made.

His influence on such composers as Ravel and Louis Aubert, and even indirectly through another pupil, Nadia Boulanger, on the later generation of musicians of her school, was that of a master by whose example, more almost than any other, French music had recovered from nineteenth-century mediocrity without falling into revolutionary extravagance. He was indeed more seminal for the future of music than many who advertised their futurism on the surface; certainly his following has had a very different history from that of the post-Wagnerians such as Richard Strauss or the latter-day romantics like Mahler—a double strain which either petered out in the frustrated strivings of Schreker or was driven to atonal experimentation for which even Alban Berg was not able to provide a quite undeniable direction.

The fruit of Fauré's fertilizing influence on music has yet, I think, to ripen; none of his pupils, not even Ravel, was a

[1] A term frequently applied in the later nineteenth century to Verlaine and other poets of both the Parnassian and the Symbolist schools. See p. 77.

[2] A reference to the first line of *Clair de lune*.

[3] *La Revue musicale*, December 1924.

composer of more than secondary rank, but on the other hand the lines he laid down for musical development will be, and are indeed already proving, more indispensable for the guidance of a still later generation than those, perhaps, of Franck, or for that matter of many no less genuine leaders of musical reawakening outside France, whom Fauré himself would have been one of the first to salute. The long reach of his significance for the future is of a piece with the extent of his roots in musical history; he was less overshadowed than most of his contemporaries by the immediate past, and he left on record his adherence to this valuable principle: 'To know an art really well, one should not be ignorant of any part of its origins or of its development'.[1] The teaching done under his direction, in which the notion of musical classics was at last freed from its exclusive identification with a single phase of the art; the efforts he made as president of the S.M.I. to give the concert world as well focussed a musical perspective as his own—all this is intimately allied with his achievement as a composer who was modern in exact proportion to his knowledge of the ancients.

Modern—and all the more fruitful in his modernity because it had nothing in common with the kind of modernism that has no roots. The 'transvaluation of values' implicit in Hindemith's *Gebrauchsmusik* or in Jean Cocteau's demand for 'everyday music' had no place in his scheme of things. He never, says his son[2], wrote out of mere facility or by way of exercising his skill; he would not even, I think, have conceded so much to the pure craftsman as to subscribe to Rimsky-Korsakov's principle of writing regularly in order to keep oneself in training. He does not appear to have left very much unpublished (the main exceptions have already been noted, and there remains only to add to them another set of incidental theatre music, for a play *Le Voile du bonheur* by Georges Clemenceau); nor did he hesitate to lie fallow when he had nothing of importance to say. And with this he nevertheless attained a total of 121 opus numbers in which the proportion of 'roughage' is remarkably small; perhaps because

1 Reported by P. Fauré-Fremiet, *op. cit.*, p. 68.

2 *Op. cit.*, p. 29.

he had a specific reason for composing each one of them. Music for him was something to be written, and performed, with deliberate purposefulness; artistic imagination, he once wrote,

> consists in giving a shape to the best of what one would like to exist—to whatever surpasses ordinary reality. Do not therefore be afraid to hazard what may afterwards seem to you absurd; it will still not be time wasted. The essence of musical art consists, to my mind, in raising us as far as possible above things as they are.[1]

An outlook which must be carefully distinguished from romantic 'exaltation', for it is the exact opposite of a willing servitude to one's subconscious impulses. Fauré could set himself out to perform, or even to compose, without waiting to be seized by a mood. He once dragged Jacques Thibaud out to an evening party where they were expected to make music, regardless of the fact that the violinist had already gone to bed with a temperature[2]. And he demanded something of the same docility from his own faculty as a composer:

> Fauré constantly thought in terms of music; but a melodic and harmonic substance had to be given to these thoughts—that is what is meant by the labour of composition. The word 'Inspiration', with a capital letter, simply made him smile.[3]

Somebody once asked him in what wonderful surroundings he had got the inspiration for his sixth Nocturne, and he replied gravely: 'In the Simplon tunnel.'[4] Lover of fine scenery though he was, he did not try to derive mystical 'correspondences' from it; and though I have suggested elsewhere[5] a resemblance between the music of his final period and the surroundings in which he wrote it, I should not wish my remark to be interpreted as implying a relation of cause and effect. Clearly Fauré did not rely on external influences for his inspirations, nor suppose that

[1] *Ibid.*, pl. XLI (reproduction of a manuscript).

[2] *Ibid.*, p. 55.

[3] *Ibid.*, pp. 29-30.

[4] *Ibid.*, p. 53.

[5] See p. 118.

musical invention would come of an excited, sentimental reaction to his surroundings or his experiences. At the same time he did not fall into the contrary error of supposing that sheer industry will discover the primary musical matter which it is its function to develop. The nearest approach I have seen to his notion of artistic inspiration is that of certain French thinkers of the early eighteenth century, such as Fontenelle, who also was so suspicious of the common theory of 'inspiration' that he avoided the word and used 'talent' instead, defining it as 'the natural motion which directs our attention with effortless accuracy upon certain objects, and causes us to apprehend them correctly without any need of reflexion'[1]; but which needs to be supplemented by reflective effort (Fontenelle called it *esprit*, a word that has no complete equivalent in English) in order that from these initial apprehensions shall be derived that *design of ideas* which we call artistic form. Perhaps an even more apt illustration of the outlook I am trying to describe is provided by the celebrated connoisseur and patron of the arts, the Comte de Caylus, one of whose Academy addresses in 1747 is thus reported by his biographer:

> What, in the estimation of Caylus, made an artist? To begin with, an uncommon subtlety of sense-perception, no more, no less. . . . 'Natural gifts consist simply of greater aptitude in one person than in another to receive impressions and allow them to germinate.'[2]

To seize thus upon significances of sound, and to 'combine them in peculiar and unexpected ways'[3]—this, it may be deduced, was the process of composition as Fauré understood it.

All of which points to the central fact, that he was the opposite of a romantic; especially because his music was intended to convey a meaning inherent in its own form, and not any extra-

[1] From an essay, *Sur la poésie en général*, quoted by Monglond, *Le Préromantisme français*, Vol. I, p. 31.

[2] S. Rocheblave, *Essai sur le comte de Caylus*, p. 177. The mixed metaphor is Caylus's, not mine.

[3] See p. 126, n.

neous message, not even—or least of all—personal confidences from the world of his own passions and sentiments. His art, like his own nature, was never effusive; it might almost be said of him, I think, as it was said of Alfred de Vigny, that no one enjoyed his most intimate confidence—not even his family, which is why I have considered myself at liberty to disagree with one or two of the judgments passed on his moral dispositions by his son. It is an excellent qualification of his music to describe it, with M. Jean Chantavoine, as 'unrelated to anything that was not pure music, the reflexion of his mind in sound', provided we remember that the word *reflexion* here carries its fullest sense: that Fauré's mind reflected upon the objects presenting themselves to it and did not project his personal nature into them. His musical language, further described by the same critic as supremely responsive 'to the fleeting shapes of each successive impression, and to each wave by which it was aroused to a vibration *that never became febrile*'[1], does not seek to call attention to himself rather than to his product. The subjective purpose in art will find no guarantee in Fauré; 'his most pleasing meditations never degenerate into Fichte's travesty of poetry as "the dream of a dream" '.[2] However subjective the experiences that may have led him to his artistic discoveries, they are not perpetuated in them; and the sentimental hearer who can be moved only by external evidence of emotion will find his art unprofitable. For it has been epitomized finally by Mlle. Nadia Boulanger as the art of one who 'was guided by his feelings themselves to set reason upon his altar'.[3]

This Hellenic quality is eminently appropriate to a composer who embodied a new Greek illumination for music, in that he

[1] J. Chantavoine, in the *Ménestrel*, 13th June 1922. The italics are mine.

[2] Georges Auric, in *La Revue musicale*, December 1924.

[3] *La Revue musicale*, October 1922. I think Mlle. Boulanger was here making a further adaptation from Maurras, whose account of the ancient Athenians is as follows: 'Feeling was the spring of all their behaviour, and it was reason that they set upon their altar. The event is the greatest in the history of the world.' (*Anthinéa*, p. 103.)

helped in France to redress the balance weighed down by German music, which his example may yet contribute to place in its proper perspective for the rest of the western world. 'Reason upon his altar'—does not this perfectly express the standpoint of those elect people of the ancient world for whom experience presented, above all, opportunities of comprehension[1], so that it is to their example we return with relief from each successive attack of irrational sensibility and passion admired for its own sake? And does not Fauré's music answer perfectly to this description of the Hellenic rational serenity, since it expresses, supremely and exclusively, comprehension by the human mind of the varied objects of its attention, and is for that very reason blamed as 'expressionless' by those who can find expressiveness only in self-exhibition? The 'pith and marrow of his attribute' is offered to us with the minimum of external attractions; his music, more than many other composers', will not yield its meaning to those who give it only a part of their attention.[2] Neither does it force itself on the sense by pretensions to 'colourful' appeal or to 'soul', but waits, like Mozart's, for listeners who will meet it with an ear tuned to the reception of its musical, not sentimental, design. It may justly be compared to a fine wine, which of all liquors recommends itself by the unaided quality of its flavour and *bouquet*. Beer of an inferior standard may sometimes be temporarily acceptable because of its sheer gravity—an image which may without irreverence be applied to the work of Wagner at its lower levels; and spirituous liquors can at times serve a desired purpose by sheer headiness—which is true of some of the lesser Russian compositions, even some of Mussorgsky's. But Fauré stands or falls by musical invention alone. His music, aristocratic in its disdain to compete for favour, Hellenic in the splendid finality of its resolution of material into form, is worthy of a place among the greatest masterpieces because it offers none but the most genuine credentials for admission to their company.

[1] See p. 103, n.

[2] Koechlin, *op. cit.*, p. 202, n.

APPENDICES

APPENDIX A

CALENDAR

(*Figures in parentheses denote the age reached by the person mentioned during the year in question.*)

Year	*Age*	*Life*	*Contemporary Musicians*
1845		Gabriel Urbain Fauré born, May 12, at Pamiers, Dept. of Ariège, son of Toussaint-Honoré Fauré, a schoolmaster. The child is put out to nurse at the village of Verniolles and, there being 5 elder children, he is left there for 4 years.	Widor born, Feb. 22. Adam aged 42; Alkan 32; Auber 63; Balakirev 9; Balfe 37; Benedict 41; Bishop 59; Bizet 7; Boito 3; Borodin 11; Brahms 12; Bruch 7; Bruckner 22; Castillon 7; Chabrier 4; Chopin 35; Cornelius 22; Cui 10; David (Félicien) 35; Dargomizhsky 32; Delibes 9; Donizetti 48; Dvořák 4; Flotow 33; Franck 23; Gade 28; Gevaert 17; Glinka 42; Gounod 27; Grieg 2; Guilmant 8; Halévy 54; Heller 30; Liszt 34; Lortzing 42; Massenet 3; Mendelssohn 36; Mercadante 50; Meyerbeer 54; Mussorgsky 6; Nicolai 35; Offenbach 26; Pedrell 4; Reyer 22; Rimsky-Korsakov 1; Rossini 53; Rubinstein 15; Saint-Saëns 10; Schumann 35; Smetana 22; Spohr 61; Spontini 71; Strauss (J.i) 41; Strauss (J.ii) 20; Sullivan 3; Tchaikovsky 5; Thomas (A.) 34; Verdi 32; Wagner 32.
1846	1		
1847	2		Mackenzie born, Aug. 22; Mendelssohn (38) dies, Nov. 4.
1848	3		Donizetti (51) dies, April 8; Duparc born, Jan. 21; Parry born, Feb. 27.
1849	4	Returns home to the family, now living at Montgauzy near Foix.	Chopin (39) dies, Oct. 17; Nicolai (39) dies, May 11.
1850	5		

Year	*Age*	*Life*	*Contemporary Musicians*
1851	6		d'Indy born, March 27; Lortzing (48) dies, Jan. 21; Spontini (77) dies, Jan. 14.
1852	7		Stanford born, Sept. 30.
1853	8	Is heard playing the harmonium at the village church by a blind lady, who urges his parents to let him study music.	Messager born, Dec. 30.
1854	9	F. is sent to the École Niedermeyer in Paris for musical training and general education.	Humperdinck born, Sept. 1; Janáček born, July 4.
1855	10		Bishop (69) dies, April 30; Chausson born, Jan. 21; Liadov born, May 11.
1856	11		Martucci born, Jan. 6; Schumann (46) dies, July 29; Sinding born, Jan. 11; Taneiev born, Nov. 25.
1857	12	Studies at the École Niedermeyer.	Pruneau born, March 1; Elgar born, June 2; Glinka (54) dies, Feb. 15.
1858	13		Hüe born, May 6; Leoncavallo born, March 8; Puccini born, June 22; Smyth (Ethel) born, April 23.
1859	14		Chevillard born, Oct 14; Spohr (75) dies, Oct. 22.
1860	15	Saint-Saëns (25) joins the teaching staff of the school and makes friends with F.	Albéniz born, May 28; Charpentier born, June 25; Mahler born, July 7; Wolf born, March 13.
1861	16		Bréville born, Feb. 21; Chaminade born, Aug. 8; Loeffler born, Jan. 30; MacDowell born, Dec. 18.
1862	17	Studies at the École Niedermeyer continued.	Debussy born, Aug. 22; Delius born Jan. 29; Halévy (63) dies, March 17.
1863	18	First published piano work, *Trois Romances sans paroles* (Op. 17), composed.	Mascagni born, Dec. 7; Pierné born, Aug. 16.
1864	19		Meyerbeer (73) dies, May 2; Ropartz born, June 15; Strauss (R.) born, June 11.

Appendix A

Year	*Age*	*Life*	*Contemporary Musicians*
1865	20	Leaves the École Niedermeyer. First 20 songs (Opp. 1-8) written by this time.	Dukas born, Oct. 1; Glazunov born, Aug. 10; Magnard born, June 9; Sibelius born, Dec. 8.
1866	21	Appointed organist of the church of Saint-Sauveur at Rennes, Jan.	Busoni born, April 1; Satie born, March 17.
1867	22		Granados born, July 29; Koechlin born, Nov. 27.
1868	23	Mme. Miolan-Carvalho, whom he accompanies at a concert at Rennes, sings his song *Le Papillon et la fleur*.	Bantock born, Aug. 7; Rossini (76) dies, Nov. 13.
1869	24		Berlioz (66) dies, March 8; Dargomizhsky (56) dies, Jan. 17; Pfitzner born, May 5; Roussel born, April 5.
1870	25	Dismissed from the church at Rennes, he returns to Paris and becomes organist at the church of Notre-Dame de Clignancourt, March. He joins a light infantry regiment to fight in the Franco-Prussian War.	Balfe (62) dies, Oct. 20; Mercadante (75) dies, Dec. 17; Novák born, Dec. 5; Schmitt born, Sept. 28.
1871	26	At its end, during the Communard disturbances, he takes refuge at Rambouillet. Organist at church of Saint-Honoré d'-Eylau, then becomes assistant to Widor at the church of Saint-Sulpice and sometimes deputizes for Saint-Saëns (36) at the organ of the Madeleine.	Auber (89) dies, May 12.
1872	27	Joins the teaching-staff of the École Niedermeyer.	Skriabin born, Jan. 4; Vaughan Williams born, Oct. 12.
1873	28	Falls in love with Marianne Viardot, the daughter of Pauline Viardot-Garcia (52). *Cantique de Racine* (Op. 11) for chorus and instruments.	Rakhmaninov born, April 1; Reger born, March 19; Séverac born, July 20.
1874	29	Suite in F major for orchestra (unpublished) performed at the Colonne concerts.	Cornelius (50) dies, Oct. 26; Holst born, Sept. 21; Schoenberg born, Sept. 13; Suk born, Jan. 4.

Year	*Age*	*Life*	*Contemporary Musicians*
1875	30	*Les Djinns* (Op. 12) for chorus and orchestra.	Bizet (37) dies, June 3; Coleridge-Taylor born, Aug. 15; Ravel born, March 7; Roger-Ducasse born, April 18.
1876	31	First violin Sonata, in A major, composed.	Falla born, Nov. 23; Wolf-Ferrari born, Jan. 12.
1877	32	Saint-Saëns having resigned his organist's appointment at the Madeleine in favour of Théodore Dubois, F. takes Dubois's place as assistant organist and choirmaster. He visits Liszt (66) at Weimar in the company of Saint-Saëns. He is at last accepted by Marianne Viardot, but she soon breaks off the engagement.	Dohnányi born, July 27.
1878	33	Second visit to Germany, where he hears Wagner's (65) *Rhinegold* and *Valkyrie* at Cologne. First violin Sonata performed at the Trocadéro during the Paris Exhibition.	Palmgren born, Feb. 16; Schreker born, March 23.
1879	34	First piano Quartet, C minor, composed. Visit to Munich to hear Wagner's *Ring*. Violin Concerto (first movement only not published) performed.	Bridge (Frank) born, Feb. 26; Caplet born, Nov. 27; Delage born, Nov. 13; Grovlez born, April 4; Ireland born, Aug. 13; Medtner born, Dec. 24; Respighi born, July 9; Scott (Cyril) born, Sept. 27.
1880	35	Songs Op. 18. *Berceuse* for violin and piano (Op. 16).	Bloch born, July 24; Inghelbrecht born, Sept. 17; Offenbach (61) dies, Oct. 4; Pizzetti born, Sept. 20.
1881	36	*Ballade* for piano and orchestra composed. Songs Op. 23.	Bartók born, March 25; Miaskovsky born, April 20; Mussorgsky (42) dies, March 28.
1882	37	Songs Op. 27.	Kodály born, Dec. 16; Malipiero born, March 18; Raff (60) dies, June 24-5; Stravinsky born, June 17; Turina born, Dec. 9; Vycpálek born, Feb. 23.
1883	38	Marries Marie Fremiet, daughter of the sculptor Emmanuel	Bax born, Nov. 6; Casella born, July 25; Szymanowski born,

Year	*Age*	*Life*	*Contemporary Musicians*
		Fremiet (59). Opp. 25, 26, 30-34 for piano composed. Songs Op. 39.	Sept. 21; Wagner (70) dies, Feb. 13; Webern born, Dec. 3; Zandonai born, May 28.
1884	39	Opp. 36-38 for piano.	Van Dieren born, Dec. 27; Griffes born, Sept. 17; Smetana (60) dies, May 12.
1885	40	Symphony in D minor (not preserved) performed at the Colonne concerts, March 15. Death of his father at Toulouse. Opp. 41-2 for piano.	Berg born, Feb. 7; Wellesz born, Oct. 21.
1886	41	Composition of the Requiem in memory of his father. Second piano Quartet, G minor. Op. 44 for piano. Songs Op. 43.	Kaminski born, July 4; Liszt (75) dies, July 31; Ponchielli (52) dies, Jan. 16.
1887	42	Songs Op. 46. *Pavane* for orchestra (with chorus *ad lib.*, Op. 50).	Borodin (53) dies, Feb. 28; Toch born, Dec. 7.
1888	43	First performance of the Requiem at the Madeleine. Incidental music for Dumas's *Caligula*, produced at the Odéon.	Alkan (75) dies, March 29; Durey born, May 27; Heller (74) dies, Jan. 14.
1889	44	Incidental music for Haraucourt's *Shylock*, produced at the Odéon. Songs Op. 51.	Shaporin born, Nov. 8.
1890	45	Visit to Venice, where he writes the 5 Verlaine songs (Op. 58). First piano Quintet begun, but laid aside.	Franck (68) dies, Nov. 8; Gade (73) dies, Dec. 21.
1891	46	Nine more Verlaine songs composed as a cycle, *La Bonne Chanson*. Op. 59 for piano.	Bliss born, Aug. 2; Delibes (55) dies, Jan 16; Migot born, Feb. 27; Prokofiev born, April 23; Roland-Manuel born, March 22.
1892	47	Becomes inspector of music of the state-aided conservatoires in succession to Guiraud (55), who has died May 6.	Honegger born, March 10; Jarnach born, July 26; Kilpinen born, Feb. 4; Lalo (69) dies, April 22; Milhaud born, Sept. 4; Tailleferre (Germaine) born, April 19.
1893	48	*Dolly* Suite for piano duet (Op. 56).	Goossens born, May 26; Gounod (75) dies, Oct. 18; Tchaikovsky (53) dies, Nov. 6.

Year	*Age*	*Life*	*Contemporary Musicians*
1894	49	Opp. 62-3 for piano.	Chabrier (53) dies, Sept. 13; Pijper born, Sept. 8; Rubinstein (64) dies, Nov. 20.
1895	50	Op. 66 for piano.	Castelnuovo-Tedesco born, April 13; Hindemith born, Nov. 16; Sowerby born, May 1.
1896	51	Succeeds Dubois (59) as chief organist at the Madeleine, June 2, and is appointed professor of composition at the Conservatoire, Oct. 10. Op. 70 for piano.	Bruckner (72) dies, Oct. 11; Sessions born, Dec. 28; Thomas (A.) (85) dies, Feb. 12.
1897	52	*Thème et Variations* (Op. 73) for piano. Songs Op. 76.	Brahms (64) dies, April 3; Korngold born, May 29.
1898	53	Visit to London for the production of Maeterlinck's (36) *Pelléas et Mélisande* at the Prince of Wales Theatre, for which he has been commissioned to write incidental music, June 21. Op. 74 for piano. *Papillon* and *Sicilienne* for cello and piano (Opp. 77-8).	Rieti born, Jan. 28.
1899	54		Auric born, Feb. 15; Chausson (44) dies, June 10; Poulenc born, Jan. 7; Strauss (J.ii) dies, June 3.
1900	55	Production of *Prométhée* at the open-air theatre of Béziers, Aug. 1. Songs Op. 83.	Křenek born, Aug. 23; Sullivan (58) dies, Nov. 22.
1901	56	*Prométhée* repeated at Béziers, Aug.	Verdi (88) dies, Jan. 27.
1902	57	*Huit Pièces brèves* (Op. 84) for piano completed.	Walton born, March 29.
1903	58	Invited to write musical criticism for the *Figaro*. Signs of deafness begin to show themselves. Songs Op. 85.	Wolf (43) dies, Feb. 22.
1904	59	Songs Op. 87.	Dvořák (63) dies, May 1.
1905	60	Succeeds Dubois (68) as director of the Conservatoire, June, where he gradually introduces reforms.	Lambert born, Aug. 23.
1906	61	First piano Quintet (Op. 89, see 1890) completed. Opp. 90-1 for piano. Songs Op. 92.	Arensky (45) dies, June 11; Cartan born, Dec. 1; Shostakovitch born, Sept. 25.

Appendix A

Year	*Age*	*Life*	*Contemporary Musicians*
1907	62	*Prométhée* revived at the Paris Hippodrome and then at the Opéra. The singer Lucienne Bréval (38) suggests the opera *Pénélope*. Songs Op. 94.	Grieg (64) dies, Sept. 4.
1908	63	Opp. 96-7 for piano. *Sérénade* for cello and piano (Op. 98).	MacDowell (47) dies, Jan. 24; Rimsky-Korsakov (64) dies, June 21.
1909	64	Succeeds Reyer as a member of the Institut de France. Op. 99 for piano.	Albeniz (49) dies, June 16; Bordes (46) dies, Nov. 18; Martucci (53) dies, June 1; Reyer (86) dies, Jan. 15.
1910	65	Deafness has become a serious handicap by this time. He is made *Commandeur* of the Legion of Honour. Opp. 101-2 for piano. Song cycle *La Chanson d'Ève* (Op. 95) completed.	Balakirev (74) dies, May 30.
1911	66	Nine Preludes (Op. 103) for piano completed.	Mahler (51) dies, May 18.
1912	67		Coleridge-Taylor (37) dies, Sept. 1; Massenet (70) dies, Aug. 13.
1913	68	*Pénélope* produced at Monte Carlo, March 4, and first performed in Paris, May 10. Op. 104 for piano.	
1914	69	Op. 105 for piano.	Liadov (59) dies, Aug. 28.
1915	70		Scriabin (44) dies, April 14; Taneiev (59) dies, June.
1916	71		Granados (49) dies, March 24; Reger (43) dies, May 11.
1917	72	Second Sonata for violin and piano (Op. 108).	
1918	73	First Sonata for cello and piano (Op. 109). Song cycle *Le Jardin clos* (Op. 106) completed.	Boito (76) dies, June 10; Cui (83) dies, March 14; Debussy (56) dies, March 25; Parry (70) dies, Oct. 7.
1919	74	*Fantaisie* for piano and orchestra (Op. 111). Song cycle *Mirages* (Op. 113).	Leoncavallo (61) dies, Aug. 9.
1920	75	His deafness has become so serious that he is asked to resign the directorship of the Conser-	Bruch (82) dies, Oct. 2; Griffes (36) dies, April 8.

Year	Age	Life	Contemporary Musicians
		vatoire. He is given the *grand cordon* of the Legion of Honour. *Masques et bergamasques*, suite for orchestra (Op. 112).	
1921	76	Plays for the last time at a concert, at Tours, but is unable to hear the music. Second piano Quintet (Op. 115). Op. 116 for piano.	Humperdinck (67) dies, Sept. 27; Saint-Saëns (86) dies, Dec. 16; Séverac (48) dies, March 23.
1922	77	Benefit concert at the Sorbonne, June 20. Fauré number of *La Revue musicale* published. Second Sonata for cello and piano (Op. 117). Song cycle *L'Horizon chimérique* (Op. 118). Op. 119 for piano.	Pedrell (81) dies, Aug. 19.
1923	78	String Quartet (Op. 121) begun.	
1924	79	String Quartet finished at Annecy, near Geneva, summer. He is so ill there that he has to take oxygen, and returns to Paris to be with his family. Fauré dies in Paris, Nov. 4.	Busoni (58) dies, July 27; Puccini (66) dies, Nov. 29; Stanford (72) dies, March 29. Auric aged 25; Bantock 56; Bartók 43; Bax 41; Berg 39; Bliss 33; Bloch 44; Bréville 63; Bridge (Frank) 45; Bruneau 67; Casella 41; Castelnuovo-Tedesco 29; Charpentier 64; Delius 62; van Dieren 40; Dohnányi 47; Dukas 59; Duparc 76; Durey 36; Elgar 67; Falla 48; Glazunov 59; Goossens 31; Hindemith 29; Holst 50; Honegger 32; d'Indy 73; Ireland 45; Janáček 70; Jarnach 31; Kaminski 38; Kilpinen 32; Kodály 42; Korngold 27; Křenek 24; Lambert 19; Loeffler 63; Malipiero 42; Mascagni 61; Medtner 45; Miaskovsky 43; Milhaud 32; Novák 54; Palmgren 46; Pfitzner 55; Pierné 61; Pijper 30; Pizzetti 44; Poulenc 25; Prokofiev 33; Rakhmaninov 51; Ravel 49; Respighi 45;

Year	*Age*	*Life*	*Contemporary Musicians*
			Rieti 26; Roger-Ducasse 49; Roland-Manuel 33; Ropartz 60; Roussel 55; Satie 56; Schmitt 54; Schoenberg 50; Schreker 46; Scott (Cyril) 45; Sessions 28; Shaporin 35; Shostakovitch 18; Sibelius 59; Sowerby 29; Strauss (R.) 60; Stravinsky 42; Suk 50; Szymanowski 41; Toch 37; Turina 42; Vaughan Williams 52; Vycpálek 42; Walton 22; Webern 41; Wellesz 39; Wolf-Ferrari 48; Zandonai 41.

APPENDIX B

CATALOGUE OF WORKS

(*Dates shown in italics are approximate.*)

Op. — *Dramatic Works*

52. *Caligula*, tragedy by Alexandre Dumas, incidental music (1888).
57. *Shylock*, drama after Shakespeare by Edmond Haraucourt, incidental music (1889).
80. *Pelléas et Mélisande*, drama by Maurice Maeterlinck, incidental music (1898).
82. *Prométhée*, lyric tragedy (Jean Lorrain and F. A. Hérold) (1900).
88. *Le Voile du bonheur*, play by Georges Clemenceau, incidental music (1901).
- *Pénélope*, lyric drama (René Fauchois) (1913).

Orchestral Works

20. Suite (1875, unpublished, but *see* Op. 68).
40. Symphony in D minor (1884, unpublished).
50. *Pavane*, with chorus *ad lib.* (1887).
56. *Dolly*, suite (1893-96, scored by Henri Rabaud).
68. *Allegro symphonique* (1875, No. 1 of Op. 20).
112. *Masques et bergamasques*, suite (1920).

Works for Solo Instruments and Orchestra

14. Concerto for violin and orchestra (1878, unpublished, ? unfinished).
19. *Ballade* for pianoforte and orchestra (1881, originally pianoforte alone).
28. *Romance* for violin and orchestra (1882).
111. *Fantaisie* for pianoforte and orchestra (1919).

Chamber Music

15. Quartet for violin, viola, violoncello and pianoforte in C minor (1879).
45. Quartet for violin, viola, violoncello and pianoforte in G minor (1886).
89. Quintet for pianoforte and strings in D minor (1906).
115 Quintet for pianoforte and strings in C minor (1921).
120. Trio for violin, violoncello and pianoforte in D minor (1923).
121. String quartet in E minor (1924).

Instrumental Sonatas

13. Sonata for violin and pianoforte in A major (1876).
108. Sonata for violin and pianoforte in E minor (1917).
109. Sonata for violoncello and pianoforte in D minor (1918).
117. Sonata for violoncello and pianoforte in G minor (1922).

Appendix B

Op. *Instrumental Pieces*

16. *Berceuse* for violin and pianoforte (1880).
24. *Élégie* for violoncello and pianoforte (1883).
49. *Petite Pièce* for violoncello and pianoforte (1889, unpublished).
69. *Romance* for violoncello and pianoforte (*1895*).
75. *Andante* for violin and pianoforte (1898).
77. *Papillon* for violoncello and pianoforte (1898).
78. *Sicilienne* for violoncello and pianoforte (1898).
79. *Fantaisie* for flute and pianoforte (1898).
86. *Impromptu* for harp (1904).
98. *Sérénade* for violoncello and pianoforte (1908).
110. *Une Chatelaine en sa tour* for harp (1918).

Pianoforte Solo

17. *Trois Romances sans paroles* (1863).
25. *Impromptu* No. 1 in E flat major (1883).
26. *Barcarolle* No 1 in A minor (1883).
30. *Valse-Caprice* No. 1 in A major (1883).
31. *Impromptu* No. 2 in F minor (1883).
32. *Mazurka* (1883).
33. *Nocturnes* Nos. 1-3 in E flat minor, B major and A flat major (1883).
34. *Impromptu* No. 3 in A flat major (1883).
36. *Nocturne* No. 4 in E flat major (1884)
37. *Nocturne* No. 5 in B flat major (1884).
38. *Valse-Caprice* No. 2 in D flat major (1884).
41. *Barcarolle* No. 2 in G major (1885).
42. *Barcarolle* No. 3 in G flat major (1885).
44. *Barcarolle* No. 4 in A flat major (1886).
59. *Valse-Caprice* No. 3 in G flat major (1891).
62. *Valse-Caprice* No. 4 in A flat major (1894).
63. *Nocturne* No. 6 in D flat major (*1894*).
66. *Barcarolle* No. 5 in F sharp minor (*1895*).
70. *Barcarolle* No. 6 in E flat major (1896).
73. *Thème et Variations* in C sharp minor (1897).
74. *Nocturne* No. 7 in C sharp minor (1898).
84. *Huit Pièces brèves* (including *Nocturne* No. 8 in D flat major, 1898-1902).

86 bis. *Impromptu* No. 6 in D flat major, transcribed from *Impromptu* for harp (1904-1913).

90. *Barcarolle* No. 7 in D minor (1906).
91. *Impromptu* No. 4 in D flat=C sharp major (1906).
96. *Barcarolle* No. 8 in D flat major (1908).
97. *Nocturne* No. 9 in B minor-major (1908).
99. *Nocturne* No. 10 in E minor (1909).

Op.
101. *Barcarolle* No. 9 in A minor (1910).
102. *Impromptu* No. 5 in F sharp minor (1910).
103. *Neuf Préludes* (1910-11).
104. 1. *Nocturne* No. 11 in F sharp minor (1913).
 2. *Barcarolle* No. 10 in A minor (1913).
105. 1. *Barcarolle* No. 11 in G minor (1914).
 2. *Barcarolle* No. 12 in E flat major (1916).
107. *Nocturne* No. 12 in E minor (1916).
116. *Barcarolle* No. 13 in C major (1921).
119. *Nocturne* No. 13 in B minor (1922).

Pianoforte Duet

56. *Dolly*, suite (1893-96):
 1. *Berceuse.*
 2. *Mi-a-ou.*
 3. *Le Jardin de Dolly.*
 4. *Kitty-Valse.*
 5. *Tendresse.*
 6. *Le Pas espagnol.*

Church Music

47. 2 Offertories (*1887*):
 1. *O Salutaris* for one voice with organ.
 2. *Maria, Mater gratiæ* for 2 voices with organ.
48. *Messe de Requiem* for soprano and baritone solo, chorus, orchestra and organ (1887).
54. *Ecce fidelis servus* for soprano, tenor and baritone with organ and double bass (*1890*).
55. *Tantum ergo* for solo and chorus (*1890*).
65. 2 Offertories (*1894*):
 1. *Ave, verum corpus* for 2 female voices, solo or chorus.
 2. *Tantum ergo* for 3-part female chorus with solos.
67. 2 Offertories (*1895*):
 1. *Salve Regina* for 1 voice with organ.
 2. *Ave Maria* for 1 voice with organ.
93. *Ave Maria* for 2 voices with organ (1906).
— *Messe basse* for 3 female voices and organ (early work, published 1907).
— *Tantum ergo* for soprano or tenor and chorus (?). 1905 according to Koechlin.
— *Tu es Petrus* for baritone solo and chorus (?). 1884 according to Koechlin.

Appendix B

Secular Vocal Works

Op.

10. 2 Duets for 2 sopranos (*1870*):
    1. *Puisqu' ici-bas* (Victor Hugo).
    2. *Tarentelle* (Marc Monnier).

11. *Cantique de Jean Racine* for chorus with harmonium and string quartet, or orchestra (*1873*).

12. *Les Djinns* (Victor Hugo) for chorus and orchestra (*1875*).
    (The above two works are probably older than the dates given.)

22. *Le Ruisseau* (anon.) for 2-part female chorus (1881).

29. *La Naissance de Vénus* (Paul Collin) for solo voices, chorus and orchestra (1882).

35. *Madrigal* (Armand Silvestre) for vocal quartet or chorus and orchestra (1884).

50. *Pavane* (anon.) for chorus *ad lib.* and orchestra (1887).

72. *Pleurs d'or* (Albert Samain) for mezzo-soprano and baritone (*1896*).

Songs

1. 2 Songs (Victor Hugo) (*1865*):
    1. *Le Papillon et la fleur.*
    2. *Mai.*

2. 2 Songs (*1865*):
    1. *Dans les Ruines d'une abbaye* (Victor Hugo).
    2. *Les Matelots* (Théophile Gautier).

3. 2 Songs (*1865*):
    1. *Seule !* (Théophile Gautier).
    2. *Sérénade toscane* (Romain Bussine).

4. 2 Songs (*1865*):
    1. *Chanson du pêcheur* (Théophile Gautier).
    2. *Lydia* (Leconte de Lisle).

5. 3 Songs (*1865*):
    1. *Chant d'automne* (Charles Baudelaire).
    2. *Rêve d'amour* (Victor Hugo).
    3. *L'Absent* (Victor Hugo).

6. 3 Songs (*1865*):
    1. *Aubade* (Louis Pommey).
    2. *Tristesse* (Théophile Gautier).
    3. *Sylvie* (Paul de Choudens).

7. 3 Songs (*1865*):
    1. *Après un rêve* (Romain Bussine).
    2. *Hymne* (Charles Baudelaire).
    3. *Barcarolle* (Marc Monnier).

Op.

8. 3 Songs (*1865*):
   1. *Au Bord de l'eau* (Armand Sully-Prudhomme).
   2. *La Rançon* (Charles Baudelaire).
   3. *Ici-bas* (Armand Sully-Prudhomme).

   (The dates of the above are approximate.

18. 3 Songs (*1880*):
   1. *Nell* (Leconte de Lisle).
   2. *Le Voyageur* (Armand Silvestre).
   3. *Automne* (Armand Silvestre).

21. *Poème d'un jour* (Charles Grandmougin) (1881):
   1. *Rencontre.*
   2. *Toujours.*
   3. *Adieu.*

23. 3 Songs (1882):
   1. *Les Berceaux* (Armand Sully-Prudhomme).
   2. *Notre Amour* (Armand Silvestre).
   3. *Le Secret* (Armand Silvestre).

27. 2 Songs (Armand Silvestre) (1883):
   1. *Chanson d'amour.*
   2. *La Fée aux chansons.*

39. 4 Songs (1884):
   1. *Aurore* (Armand Silvestre).
   2. *Fleur jetée* (Armand Silvestre).
   3. *Le Pays des rêves* (Armand Silvestre).
   4. *Les Roses d'Ispahan* (Leconte de Lisle).

43. 2 Songs (1886):
   1. *Noël* (Victor Wilder).
   2. *Nocturne* (Villiers de l'Isle-Adam).

46. 2 Songs (1887):
   1. *Les Présents* (Villiers de l'Isle-Adam).
   2. *Clair de lune* (Paul Verlaine).

51. 4 Songs (*1889*):
   1. *Larmes* (Jean Richepin).
   2. *Au Cimetière* (Jean Richepin).
   3. *Spleen* (Paul Verlaine).
   4. *La Rose* (Leconte de Lisle).

58. *Cinq Mélodies* (Paul Verlaine) (1890):
   1. *Mandoline.*
   2. *En Sourdine.*
   3. *Green.*
   4. *À Clymène.*
   5. *C'est l'extase.*

Op.

61. *La Bonne Chanson* (Paul Verlaine) (1891-92):
    1. *Une Sainte en son auréole.*
    2. *Puisque l'aube grandit.*
    3. *La lune blanche luit dans les bois.*
    4. *J'allais par des chemins perfides.*
    5. *J'ai presque peur en vérité.*
    6. *Avant que tu ne t'en ailles.*
    7. *Donc ce sera par un clair jour d'été.*
    8. *N'est-ce pas?*
    9. *L'Hiver a cessé.*

76. 2 Songs (1897):
    1 *Le Parfum impérissable* (Leconte de Lisle).
    2. *Arpège* (Albert Samain).

83. 2 Songs (1900):
    1. *Prison* (Paul Verlaine).
    2 *Soir* (Albert Samain).

85. 3 Songs (1903):
    1 *Dans la forêt de septembre* (Catulle Mendès).
    2. *La Fleur qui va sur l'eau* (Catulle Mendès).
    3. *Accompagnement* (Albert Samain).

87. *Le Plus Doux Chemin* (Armand Silvestre) (1904).

— *Le Ramier* (Armand Silvestre) (1904).

92. *Le Don silencieux* (Jean Dominique) (1906).

94. *Chanson* (Henri de Régnier) (1907).

— *Vocalise* (without words) (1907).

95. *La Chanson d'Ève* (Charles van Lerberghe) (1907-10):
    1. *Paradis.*
    2. *Prima verba*
    3. *Roses ardentes.*
    4. *Comme Dieu rayonne.*
    5. *L'Aube blanche.*
    6. *Eau vivante.*
    7. *Veilles-tu, ma senteur de soleil?*
    8. *Dans un parfum de roses blanches.*
    9. *Crépuscule.*
    10. *O Mort, poussière d'étoiles.*

106. *Le Jardin clos* (Charles van Lerberghe) (1915-18):
    1. *Exaucement.*
    2. *Quand tu plonges tes yeux dans mes yeux.*
    3. *La Messagère.*
    4. *Je me poserai sur ton cœur.*
    5. *Dans la nymphée.*
    6. *Dans la pénombre.*
    7. *Il m'est cher, Amour.*
    8. *Inscription sur le sable.*

Op.

113. *Mirages* (Baronne de Brimont) (1919):
    1. *Cygne sur l'eau.*
    2. *Reflets dans l'eau.*
    3. *Jardin nocturne.*
    4. *Danseuse.*

114. *C'est la paix* (Georgette Debladis) (1919-20).

118. *L'Horizon chimérique* (Jean de la Ville de Mirmont) (1922):
    1. *La Mer est infinie.*
    2. *Je me suis embarqué.*
    3. *Diane, Séléné.*
    4. *Vaisseaux, nous vous aurons aimés.*

— *En Prière* (Stéphane Bordèse) (1890).

APPENDIX C

PERSONALIA

Aubert, Louis (born 1877), French composer, pupil of Diémer, Lavignac and Fauré at the Paris Conservatoire. Except for an organist's post, he never held any official position. His chief work is the opera *La Forêt bleue*.

Bardac, Emma (*née Moyse*), French singer. She was the wife of a financier, from whom she obtained a divorce in order to become the second wife of Debussy, who was also divorced from his first wife, Rosalie (Lily) Texier. Emma Bardac was apparently the first to sing Fauré's song cycle *La Bonne Chanson*.

Benoit, Peter (*Pierre*) *Léopold Léonard* (1834–1901), Belgian composer who studied at the Brussels Conservatoire and later in Germany, and as a representative of the Flemish movement wrote operas, oratorios and cantatas in that language.

Bordes, Charles (1863–1909), French composer, teacher and organist. Pupil of Franck and with d'Indy and Guilmant one of the founders of the Schola Cantorum in Paris in 1894.

Boulanger, Nadia (born 1887), French teacher of composition who has attracted an international following of pupils to Paris.

Bourgault-Ducoudray, Louis Albert (1840–1910), French composer and folk-song collector. He taught at the Paris Conservatoire for thirty years and collected folk music in Greece, Scotland and Wales as well as in France, and based some of his compositions on its material.

Bréval, Lucienne (1869–1935), French soprano singer of Swiss origin and born in Berlin. Studied at Geneva and Paris and sang at the Paris Opéra for nearly thirty years.

Büsser, Henri (born 1872), French composer, organist and conductor, pupil of Widor, Gounod and Franck.

Bussine, Romain (1830–99), French singing-teacher, professor at the Paris Conservatoire. He wrote the French words for two of Fauré's songs based on Italian poems, Op. 3, No. 2, and Op. 7, No. 1.

Calvocoressi, Michael Dimitri (1877–1944), English critic of Greek descent, born and educated in France. He settled in London after the war of 1914–18 and became naturalized. Contributor of the volume on Mussorgsky to this series.

Castillon, Alexis de (1838–73), French composer, pupil of Massé and Franck. A wealthy aristocrat, he never held any official position.

Cortot, Alfred (born 1877), French pianist, born in Switzerland. Studied at the Paris Conservatoire, became a very successful concert artist and founded a trio with Casals and Thibaud.

Croiza, Claire (1882–1946), French mezzo-soprano singer, professor at the Paris Conservatoire. Although she sang in opera, including the title-part in Fauré's *Pénélope*, she was mainly a concert artist.

Dubois, Théodore (1837–1924), French composer, organist and educationist. Studied with Ambroise Thomas at the Paris Conservatoire and gained the Prix de Rome, later becoming a professor and director of the Conservatoire, as well as organist at the Madeleine.

Fauchois, René (born 1882), French actor and dramatist. He wrote plays on the lives of Mozart, Beethoven and Rossini, also comedies, one of which, *Prenez garde à la peinture,* was adapted by Emlyn Williams as *The Late Christopher Bean.* Fauchois supplied the libretto for Fauré's *Pénélope* and the scenario for his *Masques et bergamasques.*

Faure, Jean Baptiste (1830–1914), French baritone singer, student at the Paris Conservatoire, attached to the Opéra and a minor composer of songs.

Gaubert, Philippe (born 1879), French conductor and composer. Studied at the Paris Conservatoire and took the Prix de Rome. Conductor of the Conservatoire Concerts and the Opéra.

Gédalge, André (1856–1926), French composer and teacher. Student and later professor at the Paris Conservatoire.

Gigout, Eugène (1844–1925), French organist and composer. Student and later professor at Niedermeyer's school in Paris, afterwards professor at the Conservatoire and organist at Saint-Augustin.

Grovlez, Gabriel (1879–1944), French conductor and composer. Student at the Paris Conservatoire, later piano professor at the Schola Cantorum and conductor at the Opéra.

Guiraud, Ernest (1837–92), French composer and teacher. Took the Prix de Rome at the Paris Conservatoire and later became professor of composition there.

Koechlin, Charles (born 1867), French composer and critic, pupil of Massenet and Fauré.

Lalo, Pierre (born 1866), French critic, son of the composer Édouard Lalo (1823–92). Attached first to the *Journal des Débats* and later to *Le Temps.*

Lenepveu, Charles Ferdinand (1840–1910), French composer. Studied at the Paris Conservatoire, where he took the Prix de Rome and later became a professor.

Maurin, Jean Pierre (1822–94), French violinist, student and later professor at the Paris Conservatoire.

Messager, André (1853–1929), French composer and conductor. Pupil of Saint-Saëns, wrote many ballets and operettas, and conductor both at the Opéra and the Opéra-Comique.

Niedermeyer, Abraham Louis (1802–61), Swiss composer and pedagogue. Studied in Vienna, Rome and Naples, settled in Paris in 1823 and founded a school of music of his own there.

Panzéra, Charles Auguste Louis (born 1896), Swiss baritone singer. Studied at the Paris Conservatoire and settled there, sang at the Opéra-Comique, but devoted himself mainly to concert work.

Polignac, Princesse Edmond de (*Wennaretta Singer*) (1865–1943), Franco-American patroness of the arts. Born in New York and brought up in Paris and in England, she married in 1893 the Prince Edmond de Polignac (died 1901) and was both an artist herself and the hostess of a *salon* for artists.

Rabaud, Henri (born 1873), French composer and conductor. Pupil of

Massenet at the Paris Conservatoire, where he won the Prix de Rome and succeeded Fauré as director in 1920.

Reyer, Ernest (1823–1909), French composer and critic. Studied at Marseilles and Algiers and settled in Paris in 1848, where he succeeded d'Ortigues as critic of the *Journal des Débats* and Berlioz as librarian at the Conservatoire. He wrote several operas on a large scale.

Roger-Ducasse, Jean Jules (born 1873), French composer. Pupil of Fauré at the Paris Conservatoire, where he won the Prix de Rome. Later he became inspector of singing at the Paris schools.

Schmitt, Florent (born 1870), French composer. Studied at Nancy and at the Paris Conservatoire, where Fauré was among his masters, and he obtained the Prix de Rome there. Except for being director of the Lyons Conservatoire for two years, he has held no official posts.

Thibaud, Jacques (born 1880), French violinist. Studied at the Paris Conservatoire under Marsick, joined Colonne's orchestra, later toured much and formed a trio with Cortot and Casals.

Viardot-Garcia, Michelle Fernande Pauline (1821–1910), Franco-Spanish mezzo-soprano singer. Studied under her father, Manuel Garcia, and made her first appearance at Brussels in 1837.

Vuillermoz, Émile (born 1878), French critic. Studied at Lyons and under Fauré at the Paris Conservatoire. He became critic of *L'Excelsior* in 1911.

APPENDIX D

BIBLIOGRAPHY

Aguettant, L., 'Fauré' (Lyons, 1924).
Bruneau, Alfred, 'La Vie et les œuvres de Gabriel Fauré' (Paris, 1929).
Chantavoine, Jean, articles in *Le Ménestrel*, 13th and 16th June, 1922, and 14th November, 1924.
Copland, Aaron, article in *The Musical Quarterly*, October, 1924.
Cortot, Alfred, 'French Piano Music': First Series. Translated by Hilda Andrews, pp. 109–39. (Oxford, 1932.)
Dumesnil, René, 'Portraits de musiciens français,' pp. 77–98 (Paris, 1938.)
Faure [*sic*], *Gabriel*, 'Gabriel Fauré' (Paris & Grenoble, 1946).
Fauré, Gabriel, 'Opinions musicales' (Paris, 1930).
Fauré-Fremiet, Philippe, 'Gabriel Fauré' (Paris, 1929).
Hill, Edward Burlingame, 'Modern French Music'.
Jankélévitch, Vladimir, 'Gabriel Fauré et ses mélodies' (Paris, 1938).
Koechlin, Charles, 'Fauré' (Paris, 1927).
Lalo, Pierre, articles in *Le Temps*, 5th October, 1900; 22nd August, 17th October and 21st November, 1905; 31st August, 1910; and other dates.
Nouvelle Revue, La, article by J. Saint-Jean, Vol. xiii, p. 263 ff. (Paris, 1910.)
Revue Musicale, La, Fauré number. (Paris, 1922.)
Rostand, Claude, 'La Vie et l'œuvre de Gabriel Fauré' (Paris, 1945).
Schmitt, Florent, article in *Cobbett's Cyclopædic Survey of Chamber Music* (Oxford, 1929).
Séré, Octave, 'Musiciens français d'aujourd'hui, pp. 183–98. (Paris, 1921.)
Servières, G., 'Fauré' (Paris, 1930).
Vuillemin, Louis, 'Gabriel Fauré et son œuvre' (Paris, 1914).

INDEX

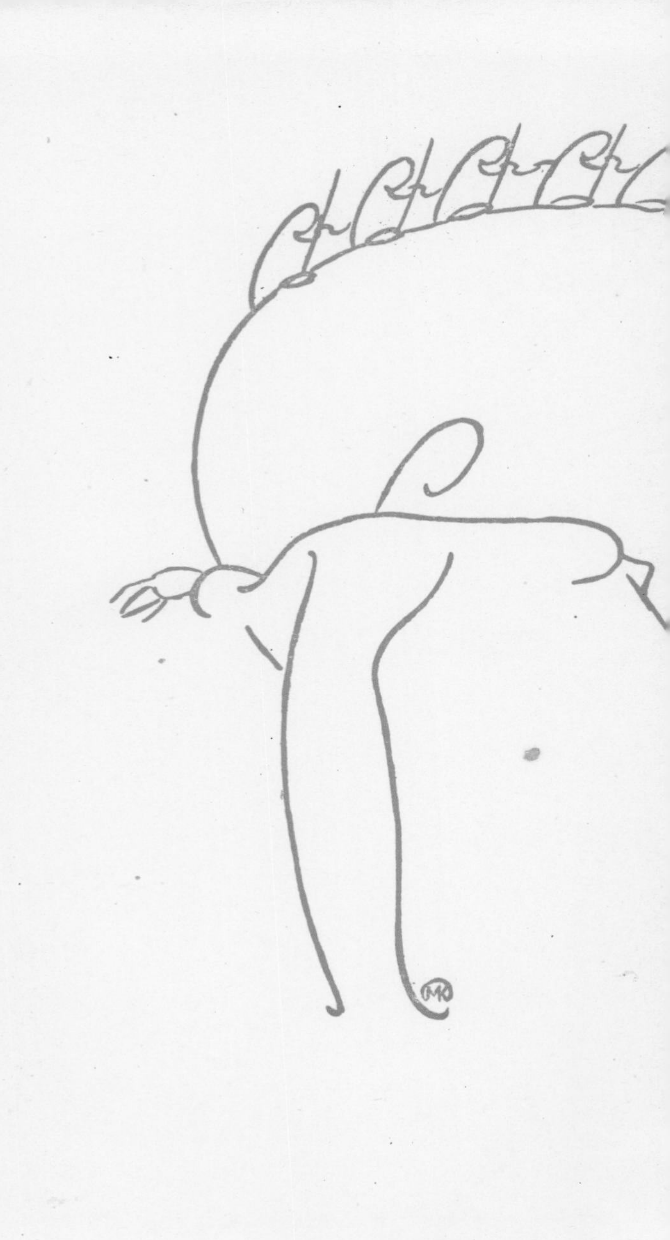